To "Mary

"were" Philly while

The Journey

A Legacy of a Life Well Lived

Orinda [*Paulson*] Koukal

Kayto & Co. Publishing
Minneapolis | Minnesota | USA

Handwritten inscription:

To "Mary

I "were" Philly & Roger while

were a part of their lives
what a blessing
they have been to so
many lives — but especially
ours. Thanks for sharing
your parents.

In Him
Rindy Is. 26:3

The Journey

A Legacy of a Life Well Lived

Orinda [*Paulson*] Koukal

Kayto & Co. Publishing
Minneapolis | Minnesota | USA

The Journey
A Legacy of a Life Well Lived

Copyright © 2022
Orinda Koukal
Kayto & Co. Publishing
ALL RIGHTS RESERVED

Cover Art: Jason Christenson

Library of Congress Control Number: 2022904427

ISBN-13: 978-1-7375276-2-6

Scriptures are taken from the KING JAMES VERSION (KJV): KING JAMES VERSION, public domain.

For more information, to request permissions, or to contact the author, please email rapidrindy@yahoo.com.

Dedication

This book is dedicated to my Sovereign Lord.

In memory of
Roger Owen Paulson
Loving Husband, Faithful Servant

May the words of this book not only be a blessing to those who read it, but inspire them to seek a deeper relationship with their Savior, Jesus Christ.

Special Thanks

Special thanks to my encouragers who prayerfully pushed me down the path of writing and publishing. I am particularly thankful for Becky Christenson, Jan Olson, and Marlys Meyers (who left for heaven before the book was finished).

I also thank my gifted publishers from *Kayto & Co. Publishing*. Well done!

Lastly, deep gratitude to my husband, Don, who gave me the "green light" to write and then tolerated my typing in seclusion. He is my KNIGHT!

Table of Contents

Chapter 1

The Beginning

Once upon a time, in a land called Single-hood, there lived a lovely, insecure, not-so-young Maiden, who loved her Lord. She felt difficulty experiencing His love as a heavenly Father, perhaps because her relationship with her earthly father was void of faithful love. Several years would pass before a birthday card would show up, without warning, full of demonstrative words of affection:

"How is my little darling? My sweet, sweet little girl. Your Daddy loves you!"

She would wonder, "Does Daddy really love me? How do I know God loves me?"

She found "love" confusing. Divorce and family bitterness had robbed her of the feeling of being cared for. Once a month, as a small child, she and her sister would take the bus with their mother to the other side of town. Financially, it was a sacrifice as the trip cost as much as a loaf of bread. Since the court ordered it, their mother faithfully performed her duty to present the girls to their father. Daddy met them at the Como Park bus stop wearing a big grin. As the girls jumped off the bus, Daddy wrapped them in his arms with a happy greeting, "How're my little darlings?"

Mother tagged along as Daddy danced down the sidewalk with the girls. It all seemed like a fairytale. The popcorn wagon was always stationed by the entrance to the pavilion where two huge stone lions perched. Daddy took pictures of the girls straddling the big cats and then he purchased the treats – peanuts for big sister and popcorn for the little one. The four of them would walk through the zoo before boarding the bus to go home. The girls would wave goodbye from the bus window. Another month would go by and everything was repeated. This continued for a few years until the child support ceased. Unfortunately, it also cancelled the face-to-face interaction with their father.

As the little Maiden grew into maidenhood, she found that she loved to be around people and especially boys and men. She craved the attention and approval that her Daddy deficit provoked. Yet, she felt very awkward around men, in general. To win their approval, she perfected entertaining conversations, silly jokes, and would always accept blatant dares.

"What?! You *DARE ME* to pyramid ski with Bruce and Glen? Sure," she would chirp.

Confident of her nimble climb up to the muscular shoulders of these avid water skiers while the boat was speeding around the lake, she enjoyed the triumph of the experience. But the not so confident dismount was not fun. Her nurse roommate examined her that evening and claimed, "Too late for stitches."

At camp she had a reputation for little tricks – like anointing the door handles and toilet seats with Vaseline, or flushing all the toilets while the gals were enjoying a nice warm shower.

Being on the PR committee for retreats gave her license for the skits. Once, to advertise what to bring, she popped out of a large trunk in a bikini holding up water skis and a towel. She loved the audience's reaction.

Having a keen mind, fair looks, shapely body, and a bubbly personality helped her win many a suitor. In fact, she never lacked for a gentleman's attention – except on a deep, deep level.

As the years passed, she aged gently and but her loneliness grew. Still, through all this, she determined to please her God. Daily, she talked to Him and read His Words in the Bible. Faithfully, she tried to measure up to His expectations. She trusted that at some future time He would reward her fervent obedience with a perfect prince who would delight her heart.

She prayed, "Dear God, teach me how to please you!"

Until HE would provide a mate for her, she would serve her God and do His bidding.

Chapter 2

The Prince Arrives

Anticipation was electric for the approaching day when the Singles were to have their annual hay ride on the Johnson Farm. The crisp autumn air and the smell of plowed under crops was a good sign that winter was arriving. You could hardly recognize the Singles as they were bundled up in heavy coats, warm hats, and mittens. The only way to find their faces was to follow their steamy breath. Yearly, the saintly, single Farmer gassed up the tractor and pulled the flatbed full of frolicking singles around his pastures until the moon was bright and the stars were like diamonds on a dark blue velvet banner. Someone would begin a chorus and the rest would join in like frogs on a log.

"Oh, when the Saints go marching in/Oh, when the saints go marching in..."

"Michael row your boat ashore, hallelujah/Michael row your boat ashore, hallelujah..."

They bellowed out the words till their voices were so hoarse that they couldn't verbally object to the other activities – like being stuffed with straw. Some were pushed off and had to run beside the rolling flatbed to be pulled back into the ruckus of hilarity. The pushing off was the most fun for the Maiden as she used her whoop-la and cunning ways to shove her suitors off, hoping to gain their focus and playful revenge. It was during this push-shove-jump back on the wagon that the Prince appeared.

Actually, he had been there all the time, passively involved with the fun. He had been singing – he knew every word. The pleasant smile on his face showed that he was enjoying observing the behaviors around him. When the pushing off began and some needed a hand, he was their ready helper. He would even jump off to help someone who fell, but then he would return to his perch. It was this act of kindness that flashed through the roar of the frolic and suspended the Prince and the Maiden in still awareness of the other's presence. You see, the Maiden was teasingly shoved off of the flatbed and reached out her hand for random help to get back on the wagon. A huge hand appeared in the dark. It belonged to the Prince. When their hands clasped in a grip of support, a warmth of gentleness flowed from his hand to hers. He then leaped off the wagon and ran beside the Maiden until he swooped her up and gently – ever so gently – perched her on the side of the hay rack. Their eyes met and she noticed him. She had never noticed before that he was brawny and well-built. Dark hair framed his gentle face and his chocolate eyes were deep and soft. They were locked with hers for an eternal second.

Truth be told that the Prince had noticed the Maiden years before. He had watched from afar and knew her flighty friendship patterns, her distinct facial features, her walk, her voice and even her sincere heart. And little did the Maiden know that the Prince had been discussing marriage with His Lord and had been investigating the inventory of damsels. Choosing to wait for His Lord's timing, he was not in pursuit of any damsel, so he, too, was pierced in his heart by the intense encounter.

Puzzled, the Maiden flipped her head and heart in another direction. She began to antagonize the damsel next to her by stuffing straw down her neck while at the same time using her feet to shove the rouge on the other side of her off the wagon. She appeared for a short time to be almost mad with emotion. But where did it come from and why did it come? Thus, the ruckus continued until the Faithful Farmer called out, "Wild Maiden, would you like to drive the tractor a bit?"

"You bet," she called back and began to make her way over the bodies and bundles of hay. Her balance on the bumpy flatbed was excellent but as she approached the Faithful Farmer her glance caught the Prince. She purposely began to campaign for cheers of approval from friends on the opposite side of the wagon. As she passed by the Prince she allowed the gentle lurch of the wagon to help her stumble. Again, his strong hand of support was there. As she allowed it to heave her forward, she lightly commented, "Thank you," not daring to meet his eyes. But, in her heart she knew she would never forget his strong hands that radiated such loving gentleness.

The Faithful Farmer stopped the hay wagon at the edge of a field and the Maiden leaped safely off the flatbed wagon and up high into the Farmer's arms. He caringly helped her climb the fender footsteps onto the tractor and then climbed up behind her to control the gears and let her delight the travelers with fancy maneuvers off the road and into the fields.

The damsels and gentlemen began singing again. How unifying, how joyous. Fun songs, silly songs, and a few serious hymns filled the night air. As the group spontaneously delivered their musical serenades, they also teased the Maiden for her weaving and wild driving. Bumping along in the night, what a merry, musical collection of light hearted country men and ladies. Little did anyone – even the Maiden – realize that this was an important beginning.

Chapter 3

The Conquest

Bible study was the next Singles event and it was here that the Maiden began to really observe the Prince. She scanned his tall, lanky outline. His feet were enormous – natural extension from his long legs. His huge hands were callused from some kind of manual labor.

"How could they look so rough and fierce and yet be so lovingly gentle?" she wondered. Long muscular arms dangled from his torso – firm, strong-looking, but not bulging.

"Was his head too large?" she thought as she examined this specimen of manhood.

"No, perfect," she concluded as she sized up his height.

"A gentle giant," she surmised. All things considered, he was a true gentleman, gracious, humble, and quiet-mannered.

She forced herself to return to reality where the swarm of Singles sat knee to knee on the floor. The Prince sat near the back, conversing quietly. He seemed to position his placement near the timid and awkward. How unlike the Maiden who flittered from one person to another like a honeybee buzzing around and collecting the nectar of nonchalant conversations from any encounter on her travels. Yes, in one evening, she could collect a snippet of surface news from almost every person.

The singing began, the chatter ceased and unity prevailed. The focus was on the song leader who opened the evening with prayer before the songs of praise and scripture. The Maiden glanced back at the Prince. He knew the words to the songs. Yes, he knew every word. She could detect his strong bass voice so confidently in tune.

"So that's who belongs to that voice," she mused. Now she knew the source of the male harmony parts that accompanied each song.

"Isn't it funny that I never noticed him before?" she thought.

After several songs, the Bible study leader encouraged everyone to collect their Bibles and notebooks. The massive group was divided and assigned to the kitchen, balcony, bedroom, and even the bathroom. It was quite a unique commotion.

Out of curiosity, the Maiden planted herself in the same group led by the Prince. Prayer to begin, then open Bibles and the lesson began. Oh my, was he prepared – really prepared. The Maiden's eyes flared when she saw his notes – so many notes!

"What does he write about?" she mused.

But the Prince offered little. He simply asked questions and inspired insights. While the Maiden responded in some way to each question or comment, the Prince quietly observed her intense interest and encouraged her to continue. Others barely had a chance to participate. Only once did the Prince genuinely participate and that was to cross reference an idea with a passage not even suggested in the lesson.

"He must really study his Bible," thought the Maiden.

He was so prepared, but he rarely volunteered his wealth of information. Yet if asked for a response, he was ready with the answer and more. Even current event clippings were a part of his study. So, the Maiden received insight into just how deep his spiritual mind was. Very deep.

The next major encounter was at the annual retreat at Lake Beauty. A summer "get away" of water skiing, hiking, basking in the sun in your favorite bathing suit, fishing for men, and a serious game of Rook. The Maiden and her court were up all night in the battle of cards and then fuzzy eyed in the morning for the spiritual speaker. She had her notebook and pen which matched her favorite and most confident outfit. Challenging concepts of holiness and surrender always pierced her heart with every word that came from the guest speakers. Wholesome and comfortable relationships provided fertile ground for deep-hearted sharing.

The Maiden just happened to be the social chairman. She fit the job because she knew everyone by name and also something interesting about them to help start a conversation. It wasn't surprising that she headed up the entertainment. Finding fools to act foolish in the skits was not always an easy job. It did, however, give her a reason to have contact. Thus, the Maiden, armed with a damsel friend, began their search for the right victims to button hole for the skit parts. The beach was bubbling with bathers, ski boats were charging across the lake, and canoes were gliding near shore with smiling faces. Sun bathers were roasting their bodies as they chit-chatted. But, there was the Prince lounging on a grassy slope overlooking the busy beach, all by himself. The damsels began to approach him to inquire about the needed parts in the play. As they snuck up for a friendly scare, the Maiden whispered to her damsel friend, "Wait, I have a better idea."

Dashing back into the camp kitchen they filled cups with water. Twittering in anticipation of their attack, the Maiden mused:

"Why does he come to retreat? All he does is read by himself. Oh well, a little weird," she concluded.

As they approached their silent victim, they failed to see the stiffening of the Prince's posture in response to their not so quiet announcement of the approaching attack.

Splash! Splash!

"Hey," responded the Prince.

Much squealing and laughter came from the Maiden and her friend, but the Prince barely reacted. He was pleasant and seemed to enjoy the fun, but was rather guarded in his response. He didn't chase the Maiden or gleefully threaten to revenge. He just stood up, towering over the damsels, and brushed the water from his hair and shoulders, chest and pants, and said, "Aaahhhhhhh – a cool splash on a hot day."

And that was it. That was it?! Then The Maiden saw that she and her damsel had doused his book – his precious distraction from single silliness.

"Well, why was he reading anyway?" she thought.

"And such a dull book – *The Customs of Israel*." Her manners surfaced and she began to apologize.

"Oh, I'm so very sorry. I didn't mean to get your book wet – Just *YOU*," she giggled. "I'll run and get a towel."

As she bounded off, she heard his booming voice, and stopped.

"No, no, that's all right. I'll just wipe it on my shirt tail. And what would you ladies be about? A little frolic, I see? You are missing the lovely lake lapping the breast of the beach under this beautiful azure umbrella of a perfect summer sky," he announced.

"My, what a poet," the Maiden retorted.

Quickly, she inquired about his willingness to be a part of the evening amusement. Much to her surprise, he agreed and she quickly knighted him as the "Running Brook." Efforts to involve the Prince in the current activities on the beach were to no avail. Even coy and coaxing proved wasted energy, so the damsel and the Maiden trotted towards the excitement of the water skiers and busy bathers.

That night, after the singing and the announcements and just before the main speaker, the traditional annual event occurred – The Camp Skit. All went as planned – the signs were taped on the victims. The "Setting Sun" appeared and kept sitting on the floor and rising up whenever the narrator spoke the words. The "Weeping Willows" cried and dabbed their eyes with hankies. The "Wind" held a broom and swept across the room blowing gently and whistling. Even the laughter was on cue until the "Running Brook." The Prince came dashing in with a bucket of water splashing helter-skelter as he jogged about the "Sun" and the "Willows." As the Prince approached the front of the stage, he reached into the bucket and showered the first few rows of the riveted audience with living, leaping, and very lively frogs. They landed on heads and laps and leaped here and there, trying to escape the clamor and chaotic capture. One landed on the Maiden's shoulder but was quickly plucked from that perch only to drop inside her garment. The Maiden jumped up and squealed, jiggling herself silly while the poor frog tried desperately to find an escape. Finally, the pursuing hand of the Maiden got a firm grip and removed the frog from the premises. The room was exploding with laughter, disgust, and amusement. What an event – never to be duplicated, for sure.

"I didn't know the Prince had a sense of humor. Very interesting," she mused.

As weeks passed into months, the Maiden continually tried to pry the Prince from his books and interest him in people and maybe even herself. He showed no interest in either.

He attended the social events but just wasn't a participant. Sitting silently in the background or talking with a loner was his favored station. He certainly wasn't a part of the action – nor did he care to be.

"Certainly," remarked the Maiden to her roommate Karen, "There's one fellow in the group I'll never marry – let alone date – and that's Sir Roger Paulson."

Little did she know that Prince Roger (who didn't know he was a Prince) had asked the King for the Maiden's hand in marriage. In fact, he had made this royal request four years prior to these recorded events. And little did the Maiden know about the notes the Prince was collecting about her – revealing things that were too hard for her to confront about herself. You see, he was an observer – as quiet as an owl in flight and as deep as an artesian well. While the Maiden was fluttering around like a whimsical butterfly, the Prince was searching hearts, gathering insights, meeting needs, and really getting to know the Singles of the Court. In his quiet, accepting way he was drawing out the inner core of those who wished to interact, giving them a beautiful part of himself. But the Maiden missed the beauty of it all. She only saw the absence of fun and gaiety – not willing to reveal her deep, heartbroken self.

Chapter 4

The Surrender

Years passed and the Maiden was pressed into another age of life and thus branded, the Lady. Time had been good to her as she still enveloped youthfulness, even in her maturity. Working with her "Little People" as a teacher, provided financial security, and much joy, not to mention the resources to explore the world. Traveling with a purpose as a short-term missionary always created an adventure. Time found her teaching in Hawaii, which was absolutely the most beautiful place on earth. But, the beauty of the landscape was scarred by harsh experiences of prejudice rebounding her to the security of the mainland. Resettled in her career, she attended several singles groups and soon found herself engaged to the wrong lad. He was demanding and over confident, believing that God had planned their marriage from the time of the Garden of Eden. The Lady was so unsure of her decisions she was sick to her stomach. Her troubled heart told her head to be strong and discontinue the relationship, but the lonely cry of single-hood engulfed her in a shadow of disappointment and despair. It was the words of God, the King of the world, that rang true, "For I know the thoughts that I think toward you, thoughts of peace and not of evil, to give you an expected end." (Jeremiah 29:11)

To obey was so hard, but she clung to those words of promise like a life line to the future.

"God has it all planned," she mused – and she broke the engagement. "Help me to trust you," she whispered inside her head to the King.

Now it wasn't that she wasn't dating – she was over-dating. A common scenario was to have a date with a different gentleman every night of the week until she would drop with exhaustion from her unhealthy schedule. Was the fear of being an unmarried older maid driving her to fill her minutes with surface relationships and avoid the real pain of loneliness? As she encountered more and more suitors, her deep feelings of incompleteness only became deeper. When she talked to God, He understood with compassion, but encouraged her again and again to wait and be content. Those two concepts were like medicinal bitter pills – wait and be content. She wanted more than a suitor or a gentleman or a night's entertainment with lovely words and gifts. She wanted a friend – a deep, intimate, loyal till death, friend. Why wouldn't the King reveal His plan to her? Why did He expect her to trust and wait?

Eager to be obedient, the Lady decided to follow God more closely. Surrendering to the King's ideas and lifestyle were frightening at first. She began to date less and spend more time with God in His Word. Daily they would talk and He would encourage her again and again to trust him. Since the Lady had no human man in her life – father, brother, uncle or male benefactor – that she could truly trust this was a difficult assignment. All male relationships had been peripheral. Promises were made, but not kept; words of encouragement and love were either not said or very sugar coated and superficial. No wonder when God spoke of His fatherly love and care for the Lady, she stiffened her heart and could not receive the gifts. But, try hard to please she did. The damsels and knights of Single-hood assured her that the King had all things planned in her best interest and over time she would slowly change into the beautiful princess that would reflect His gracious *LOVE*. She hesitantly submitted to the King's bidding.

God, the King, presented an opportunity for her to attend a Campus Crusade Christian Summer Ministry Institute in Mexico. Anticipating another adventure, she willingly packed her suitcase and left for Cuernavaca, Mexico.

Nestled inside a walled compound were the Spanish stucco buildings that comprised the Institute. Abundant birds and flowers were everywhere and seemed to decorate the monkey trees that stood in the courtyard. Cheerful warmth radiated from the daily sun as well as from the loving and caring staff. Their job was to capture the heart of the Lady and the myriad of other singles with the precepts of the Lord. Yes, this was a training ground – a preparation for the King's service. The lessons were deep. The doctrines were cognitive reflections on solid Biblical reality. Truth ripped open her hidden feelings and shed light on the inward sins that lurked unattended.

It was here that the Lady confronted her future singleness. In this beautiful setting, far away from home, she was being taught to love men as Christian brothers and allow the Lord to weave relationships of encouragement and caring support – not courtship and future fairytale bliss.

Finally, the Lady gave her desire to be married to God – allowing Him to choose her future. She became free to trust God to unfold His plan for her life. A new sense of comfortable freedom within herself developed and spilled into all of her relationships – even with men. She deeply desired to channel her energies into service wherever the Lord desired. What sweet surrender! Little did she know it was only the beginning of a plan.

While in Mexico the Lady received a friendly post card from Sir Roger. Puzzled, she said out loud to herself, "How did he know my whereabouts? I don't remember giving him this address. I haven't seen him in over a year."

The message was like a mini-Bible study and revealed that the Prince had also surrendered his life and desires to God. How strange! It almost seemed like the note came from God instead of the Prince.

Chapter 5

The King's Desire

Returning to single-hood was now frustrating. She looked at life with different eyes. She heard that the Prince was dating and that bothered her. Social events that had always inspired her, now seemed like frivolous time fillers that didn't satisfy her growing emptiness. The deep hole of loneliness inside her heart had finally surfaced – always there – nagging her, pouncing into her thoughts. She busied herself with plans and responsibilities, purposefully leaving little time to feel the hollow cave. Her King gently pointed out her tactics of avoidance and revealed how *He* could fill her emptiness with *Himself* and *His* Plans. *His* bidding became her spiritual goal. Soon she noticed that she didn't need to date or be at socials or always be surrounded by friends. Slowly she was becoming whole – the hole of emptiness was closing

– until shock ripped that black hole wide open when the Lady found out that the Prince was not only dating, but was dating a damsel of her court – a heartfelt friend. That very damsel came to the Lady and asked for advice.

"What should I do? Sir Roger keeps asking me to spend time with him and I'm really not sure. He is so quiet and socially awkward. I don't feel comfortable in public with him," she confessed.

"Well, pray about it," the Lady piously responded.

Horror, jealousy, and panic struck the Lady. But why? Wasn't it she, herself, who had spurned the Prince's gifts of homemade brownies, flowers, and hand written notes? Frequently, she found these little treasures in her P.O. Box at school. And wasn't it she who commented to the school secretary time and time again, "Was he here again? He just won't give up!"

And wasn't it the Prince who came to her apartment uninvited with a pizza for her and her roommate. The Lady was so rude and said, "You can cook it yourself, I'm leaving." And she did.

And didn't the Lady complain over and over again, "I wish he'd leave me alone," until he did stop giving her attention. And then, the Lady felt the pain of her lonely heart and ran to Her King for comfort.

Time passed and the Lady avoided the dating Damsel. That way she heard no painful information about the Prince. Since the Lady didn't like the Prince, it was such a puzzle. She would talk to herself.

"Why am I so annoyed over someone so socially backward, uninteresting, and definitely not outstanding? He also isn't charming or even dreamy to look at."

But, why did this rejection – even though it was indirect – bother her? She didn't need every man to applaud her, she surmised.

The Lady tried to dismiss her self-talk but it forced her to recognize the emptiness she still felt. In Mexico, she had chosen to trust her King with her future so this was a good opportunity to accept the Prince as just a brother.

Her current suitors became her focus. They were so brotherly and platonic from her point of view that it was certainly not a problem to keep her heart out of the relationships. However, there was one that she could easily be awestruck over. He had a kind heart, was very helpful, and was always ready to be of service. He listened to the Lady like her words were precious jewels being spewed from her mouth. His motives were pure. He served the King and desired more than anything to serve Him in active duty on the foreign field – with a wife. So noble were his desires that the Lady wondered if she would someday be his wife!? Recognizing his deep relationship with the King, she questioned him for answers.

"How do you grow spiritually, anyway?"

"Well," responded the thoughtful man, "You bathe yourself daily in God's Word. Find ways to be focused on Him during the day. KTIS Christian radio is a good time investment. Keep yourself in Bible studies, a great way to get accountability, and attend church regularly."

"What good advice," she admitted out loud. "And, how did the King become Your Lord?"

"By choice," he quickly responded. "And it will happen to you. Just put Him first."

She concluded that this man was so focused, and she was impressed, but why was her heart was so unattached? She would ask her King.

Her King seemed to always answer her indirectly which made it difficult to discern a course of action. She wanted to follow His bidding but couldn't figure it out.

"Why couldn't He give an audible, one word answer?" she would often say to herself. "Why are His answers so vague, and why couldn't He tell me which Written Words to read to find the answer?"

While studying in the book of Hosea, the words of chapter three, verse three grabbed her attention. The man Hosea tells his adulteress wife (Israel) to wait many days for *Him*.

"And I said unto her, thou shalt abide for me many days; thou shalt not play the harlot, and thou shalt not be for another man; so will I also be for thee."   - Hosea 3:3

So although the gentleman's desires and plans were noble, she just knew they did not include her and she shared this with him. He accepted graciously and they remained merry acquaintances thereafter.

The Lady remained faithful to the King's desire for her – "for peace and an expected end" (Jeremiah 29:11).

She chose to submit to His will – even if it would mean she would grow old being a Lady unchosen. Her King became her Lord.

Chapter 6

The Question

*T*he phone rang.

"It's for you," said Damsel Karen, her roommate. "It's Prince Charming," she added mockingly.

Confidently, the Lady took the phone only to find out it was Sir Roger. Mixed emotions of disappointment and anticipation flooded her heart.

"I'm returning your call about the play that's coming up. Thanks for letting me know about it. Did you call everyone in the Court?" he inquired.

"Oh yes," the Lady replied, "everyone has been notified."

"I've decided to attend," continued the Prince, "but only if you would be my guest. May I be your escort?"

Silence permeated the already chilled air of pre-winter. Then, for some reason, completely beyond her best judgement, the Lady said, "Yes."

You see, she had never accepted an invitation to a public Single Court event with a suitor. She had her reasons.

"Great!" said the Prince. "Put me down for two seats," he requested boldly. "Shall I come by for you at 7:00pm?"

"That would be fine," she automatically responded.

In a daze, the Lady put down the receiver and told Damsel Karen what she had just done. Had she just locked herself into a whole evening with Sir Roger? At this point, she did not realize he was actually *THE PRINCE* as he was the very man she vowed "never to marry – let alone date."

Her fate was sealed – she was committed. And for some strange reason, she liked it.

Wondering how her suitors would react ruffled her feathers a bit. They all knew she spent time with each of them individually, but what would they do when they saw her with studious, boring, Sir Roger? Did she really want them to see her with him? Would they think, in her advanced age as a Lady, she was getting desperate? Was it worth the risk? She would not tell a soul.

Saturday came quickly. A floor length, regal gown was carefully chosen. The ruby velvet bodice brought color to her face and was a perfect contrast to the flowered quilted skirt. She liked how the gown accentuated her tiny waist. Peeking out from the hem of the gown were her pointed silver slippers that greeted her at each step. A glance in the mirror told her that her make-up was perfect. And to finish it all off, *Vanilla Fields* perfume was applied on each wrist and behind each ear. It enveloped her body and took several minutes to evaporate. Anticipation definitely was present.

"This is only shy, quiet, uninteresting Sir Roger," she told herself. Why was she boldly accepting him as an escort in public view?

"Oh well," she mused, "people won't know we are together unless they see us get out of the carriage, and then they will think we just rode together."

There was a soft knock at the door. Damsel Karen peeked her head out of the bed chamber and mockingly chirped, "The gentleman you are never going to date or marry is at the door."

"Oh, hush," responded the Lady in teasing disgust.

She slowly paced her stride across the room and leisurely opened the door. There was Sir Roger – all decked out like a wreath on a lamp post. She scanned him top to bottom. Everything was green.

His avocado green suit accented the lighter green shirt which punctuated the multi-green cravat. The green hues made his skin look olive and contrasted so well with his jet-black hair. His chocolate eyes were twinkling and his arms were casually held behind his back.

"Good evening," the Lady politely greeted him.

"Good evening, my Lady," he chimed as he bowed gently and presented her with a box.

Her heart swelled with joy as she accepted and opened the container. A corsage of white carnations with dainty pink rose buds starred back at her – a symbol of affection. Caught off guard by the thoughtfulness, she blushed slightly. As Sir Roger gingerly helped pin on the corsage, she noticed that the dainty flowers blended well with her outfit. But her merry heart faded when she reflected on the scenario.

"Oh no," she thought, "this will be like waving a flag. Everyone knows a corsage is a signal of ownership."

She panicked, but swallowed her pride and thanked him very sweetly for the flowers. Sir Roger softly took the lacy shawl from her arm and gently wrapped it around her shoulders.

"That's strange," mused the Lady, "it seems like he has done this many times before. How many damsels has he escorted before?" she thought.

Off they sped in his old chevy, talking non-stop till the vehicle slid into a parking space and he appeared on the passenger side waiting by the open door like a footman in Cinderella. He helped her from the seat, and together they glided across the parking lot into the playhouse entrance. It all seemed wrong but felt so right. An usher led them to their seats. As they approached the group of Lords and Ladies, her heart beat faster and faster.

"I will pretend that it's planned," she told herself. "It feels like it's planned. I will not care if they match me with Sir Roger. Oooooh, Sir Roger? How unglamorous. It will be fine."

As they stumbled over legs in the long row of seated friends, there were many merry gasps and a trail of whispers. The dimming of the lights as the play began was the only thing that hushed the twittering and stopped the glances at the "new couple." The Lady soon lost herself in the characters and plot of the play and, all too soon, the evening came to a close. Like Cinderella, she felt a glow of sheer joy and yet a quiet sadness that when he walked her to the door it would be over – like a lovely dream. As they rode home, their conversation bubbled with static interest. There was a comfortable acceptance in Sir Roger that made him so easy to talk to.

Arriving at the sidewalk entrance to her abode, he offered, "May I carry you to the door, my Lady?"

"How fun," she thought and, "Why not?" she chirped back.

With that, he seemed to leap from their chevy carriage and instantly appeared at the passenger's side. He gently swooped her up into his strong arms like a pelican dips up his dinner from the rolling waves. The Lady immediately relived the love that radiated from those arms on the hay ride. She felt safe – like an eaglet caught in mid-air by a soaring parent.

Chapter 7

The Courtship

How do you express on paper the whirlwind of a fairytale relationship? Slow walks, late talks, movies, museums – all mesh into a memory of pleasant feelings. It was the very next week, after the theater event, that the Lady began to sense that something was different – that Sir Roger was so outstanding in an unidentifiable way. She began to talk to her Lord about him. A quiet confirmation about this new relationship came with a deep *PEACE* and a whispered reminder to "be still" and "trust." It seemed like her Lord delighted in the fact that the Lady had surrendered and let down her past unwritten barrier to never spend time with Sir Roger. *HIS* words continued to encourage the Lady.

"Trust in the Lord with all thine heart, and lean not unto thine own understanding."
- Proverbs 3:5

It was like God was literally telling her mind to *trust Him* to lead and allow the circumstances to develop.

The Lady whispered her questions back to her Lord.

"There must be some reason, Lord, why you desire me to know Sir Roger. It seems like I've always known him. He is so easy to be with and I feel so free – so loved. Almost like being near you, my Lord. But – what if I fall in love – then I could be spurned and rejected?"

"TRUST," said the Lord.

"I will," said the Lady. Yet inside her heart panic of abandonment shadowed her conviction.

"What shall I do if this doesn't work out?" she blurted. Her maiden friends were planning a trip to the Orient.

"Why don't you plan to come along with us?" they chirped.

"What a wonderful rescue plan," mused the Lady, "I shall have an event to look forward to and that would help me forget the pain of being abandoned by Sir Roger."

So, the Orient became her future (just in case) rescue plan. She paid a huge lump of gold to secure her reservation. You see, she didn't expect this good thing with Sir Roger to last. She had forgotten her Lord's words, "No good thing will he withhold from them that walk uprightly." (Psalm 84:11)

Well, the relationship grew deeper and deeper. The Lady recognized that the love Sir Roger had radiated from his Lord – flowing right through him to her. She knew that she was falling in love with this gentle giant and feeling a strange *PEACE* about it all.

Bible study took on a new interest for the Lady. She weekly maneuvered herself into whatever group Sir Roger attended. At first it was curiosity at Sir Roger's spiritual ideas, and then it became an awesome respect of his wisdom and insight. She recognized that his Lord and her Lord were the same person and Sir Roger knew their Lord more intimately that she did. Questions about how Sir Roger discovered and developed such deep spiritual growth gnawed at her insides.

One day she bluntly asked him, "How did you gain so much knowledge about the things of the King? And how did He become your Lord?" she asked.

"Well," he explained, "my good friend Greg had encountered Christ personally and invited Jesus into his life to be his Savior. Greg shared Christ with me and I then invited Christ into my life as well. Since my pastor disapproved of this change and all my questions, I began to search for answers in other churches and small group Bible studies. My deep thirst to know about the Bible led me to The Navigators. Their Bible studies were deep with great emphasis on memorizing scripture. I found that satisfying and helpful. The Navigators also had an intense mentoring program and I was invited to live in a Nav Home with John and Mary Hartzell, their children, and several other young men. John and Mary poured the life of Christ into each one of us. The more I grew in the Lord, the more I desired to know more and that has never changed. Oh yes, and they also taught us how to treat a lady. I've been practicing on you. How am I doing?"

He had a way of surprising people with a question, but the Lady was ready.

"I would say you are doing well in both endeavors, *BUT* a little more practice in the 'lady' department can always help. Maybe you should stay after school. I would love to help you."

This new knowledge and the fun bantering about their relationship gave her confident peace. She felt a new freedom and excitement to bare her soul to her Lord, only to find out her Lord always knew her deep inner secrets. She now felt so very comfortable in His presence and also in Sir Roger's. So strange. No need to perform or try to be accepted.

So, the first kiss was a natural event. It was also very sacred for both of them, because, through this, the Lady began to see Sir Roger as Royalty. It was an innocent kiss – the seal to a lovely evening – suspending the memory in time forever. Sir Roger gently pulled her toward him and, of course, she did not resist. Like being under a spell, she willingly surrendered her lips to his. It was an enchanting beginning to a deeper relationship. Later that evening, as she talked to her Lord in her prayer, she asked, "Is Sir Roger Your Prince?" Her Lord simply whispered, "TRUST!"

Chapter 8

The Confession

Days whirled into weeks and the Lady found herself deeper and deeper in love with Sir Roger. It was no surprise that in the middle of the roller skating floor, with couples flashing by and the waltz lights shinning their prism colors onto the floor, that Sir Roger stole a kiss and punctuated it with a fleeting confession, "I love you."

Later that evening, they both confessed their deepest feelings for each other. The world stopped... everything was suspended until... Sir Roger gently held her shoulders and locked eyes with the Lady. His face changed like pulling down a window shade and he apologized. "What have I done," he gasped. He held his head and she backed away.

"I should never have said "I love you" unless I can follow it with a marriage proposal. I want to say that – with all my heart – but this is not the right time."

And he left. As he was swept away into the darkness of night, the Lady bolted to her bed chambers and threw herself into the pillows on the bed. She wept bitterly and called out to her Lord. He was there.

"Oh Lord, I can't do this again. I can't take another broken heart. I have had enough! Remember Bud. We were pledged to each other and he went away to war and wrote me a "Dear Damsel, with great regret" letter. Then there was Bruce. Lord, we dated so long and then when I returned from the summer of missions in Mexico – there he was with Bonnie. I so wanted to keep that relationship. Why did you let me go on that Boundary Water Canoe trip that Bruce headed up? You knew he would announce his engagement to Bonnie. I could hardly find my tent because the tears were cascading down my face. But you did come to me with May-Britt as she softly patted my back while I sobbed my heart out inside my sleeping bag. How many times does my heart need to break before you cannot put it back together? Remember when I was committed to lead the singing before Bible study and Dwight called to cancel, not only our ski date, but our relationship – because he was now dating Karen. I went to Bible study anyway, with swollen eyes. My broken spirit could hardly concentrate on guitar chords or the joyful messages of the songs. Were you with me when I was sitting alone in church, silent tears gliding down my cheeks? Did you know loneliness was choking me with pain? Were you really there for me?! Every time I give my heart away, I am spurned. I don't think I can ever trust anyone!"

"Can you trust *ME?*" whispered her Lord.

"I want to. It seems too great a risk. But Lord, I'm ready. I do love Sir Roger from my deepest will. I know I would marry him if You chose him. Is he Your Prince? I need to know," she whimpered.

"Just trust," He affirmed.

"Help me to wait and trust. I will love you, Lord." She barely spoke as she drifted into an exhausting slumber.

Chapter 9

The Decision

*H*uddled inside the Lady's tiny Toyota in front of the Post Office, the couple sat praying. The car window was open level with deposit passageway into the huge official mail box. On the lady's lap was a sealed, stamped business envelope. Her hands gently caressed it like the contents were the most valuable thing she owned. Life had pushed her to a precipice of choice – trust her Lord without definite instructions or take charge of her future. She took a shaky breath as Sir Roger prayed, " Lord, help the Lady know *YOUR WILL*. Give her peace in her decision and make her path straight."

The Lady prayed in her heart, "Oh LORD, if I stay here this summer and my relationship with Sir Roger is only a temporary, will you fill my life with worthwhile things. Will you comfort my pain and help me find my security in you?"

Finally, the Lady prayed, "LORD, help me to know *YOUR WILL* for this summer and also for my future."

With that, she pulled down the levered door to the mail box and laid the lonely letter on its flat surface. As she let go of the metal flap – ever so slowly – it flipped the letter into the deep chasm. She pulled down the door again, just to be sure it was gone. It felt good! The decision was made. She would trust! Now to tell her dear damsel friends that she would not be going to the Orient. She hoped they would understand. Her reflections were interrupted by Sir Roger, "Well, my Lady, I've been praying about your decision for a different reason."

Puzzled, she looked into his twinkling eyes.

"Your mailing that cancellation letter was my confirmation that the Lord is prompting me to ask you to consider my request. Will you marry me?"

It was like a flash of lightening in the darkness. Will you marry me – marry me – marry me. Her heart began to thud. She knew what she would say. She had rehearsed it hundreds of times to her make believe prince in the mirror. Her prince. But now, Sir Roger WAS HER PRINCE – the real Prince – he had always been THE REAL PRINCE. Yes, his loving gentle manner, his sensitive thoughtful heart – how could he not be the Lord's choice. To think how blind she had been in the beginning.

"Oh, Lord," she mused, "you are so good. Again, you have given me abundantly more than I could ever think to ask you for."

"Well?"

The voice of the real Prince broke the silent seconds.

A gentle smile moved across the Lady's face as she softly said, "I should think about this – but... I already know. Yes, I will marry you. I love you so very much."

"And I love you, my darling Lady," responded the Prince.

And the decision was sealed with a tender, passionate, and holy kiss.

Chapter 10

The Testing

Weeks tumbled by providing the Prince and the Lady many activities to share. Daily they found a reason to get together. Both were full of questions for each other and lots of sharing about their families, jobs, and personal goals. Silently, the Lady was wondering about Sir Roger's commitment to his request for marriage. You see, after all these weeks, Sir Roger had still not purchased the engagement ring. Nor had he suggested that the two of them go shopping together for this "icon of commitment." The Lady dare not announce to the Singles Court their decision to wed, nor could she start the plans for the nuptial event. The worry of rejection brought out a crop of hives on her neck revealing her anxiety. She begged her Lord to help her trust *HIM* for the timing of events. She asked for a sign. Northing seemed to happen. Sir Roger suggested that besides staying involved in the Singles Bible study that they do a private Bible study together. He suggested Nehemiah.

"Strange," she thought.

But it was wonderful to steep themselves in the Lord's Word together. She didn't care as long as they were together. She loved him and wanted to be with him. And a regular commitment to be with each other gave her security.

One evening, after they had walked the three miles of Lake Harriet, they ended up in the Rose Garden.

Sir Roger bent over a huge rose and sniffed the elegant scent.

"I love the yellow roses, they remind me of God's glory," he shared.

"Let's have them as our wedding flowers?" she offered and made a mental note.

The Prince then announced, "Well, if you are going to marry me, you need to learn my favorite hymn."

"And what is that?" she asked. "Is this a test?"

"No silly," he chided. "I would just love to sing it from my heart with you," he explained. "I will help you!" he promised. "It's called, *Praise The Savior* by

Thomas Kelley, written in the early 1800s. Do you know it?"

"I've heard of it. Why do you love it?" she inquired.

"It feeds my soul every time I sing it and reminds me that God is sovereign and we can trust him," he concluded.

So, as they meandered around the rose garden he sang to her:

> *Praise the Savior, ye who know Him!*
>
> *Who can tell how much you owe Him?*
>
> *Gladly let us render to Him*
>
> *all we have and are.*

"You have a beautiful voice," she complimented, "so deep and mellow, almost celestial."

"Why, thank you!" he responded. "I will tell my Lord that you like it."

He began singing again, to her directly. She melted from his melodic message as he delivered all five verses.

When she arrived home she found her hymnal and sang the hymn to her Lord until she had memorized the words of that very verse.

Over the next few weeks, the first verse led to another. Their evening walks became duets. Their weekend day trips became a choir practice breathing music over the beauty of Minnesota. One time, as they strolled the shores of Lake Superior in Duluth, they softly sang verse two to the gentle rhythm of the waves that washed in to kiss their feet.

> *Jesus is the name that charms us;*
>
> *He for conflict fits and arms us;*
>
> *nothing moves or nothing harms us*
>
> *as we trust in Him.*

On hikes near the Light House, where cliffs were jagged and rocks under foot were unstable, the Prince would sing verse three to take their mind off the perilous path:

> *Trust in Him, ye saints, forever;*
>
> *He is faithful, changing never;*
>
> *neither force nor guile can sever*
>
> *those He loves from Him.*

Even while fixing tea for them in his Mom's kitchen, he would burst out in a verse – usually verse four:

> *Keep us, Lord, O keep us cleaving*
>
> *to Thyself and still believing,*
>
> *till the hour of our receiving*

promised joys with Thee.

So, The Lady now knew she loved a musical man as well as a deeply rooted Christian. It gave her peace. However, without notice her flaming red neck of hives would betray her. She would talk to her Lord to help her trust and now He would tell her to wait and sing.

"It's funny," mused the Lady, "how the verse I am learning at the moment seems to always fit the situation of my troubled heart."

And the Lady began to engrave the words of each verse into the surface of her soul.

ROGER OWEN PAULSON
Born September 16, 1935

Roger as a Toddler

High School Football

Boy Scouts of America, Minneapolis Troop 177

Roger's High School Graduation Portrait
1953 Columbia Heights High School

Northwestern College
1958, 1962-1965

ABOVE: Honeywell auto-pilot military training
BELOW: Roger's notes on the men in his unit

Top Row
Left to right

1. Instructor
2. McAndrew - Reg - Ohio
3. Manfred Hess - A N G - Chicago
4. Hibbert   A N G - New Jersey
5. Roger Lasko - A N G - Chicago
6. Me
7. Peter Croger - A N G - New Jersey
8. Dean Rivard - Reg - Buddette Minn
9. John Williams Reg Florida

Bottom Row
Left to Right

1. Kirkland - Reg - Ohio
2. Henry Steele - A N G - Michigan
3. Holman Dean W - A N G - Minn Farmington
4. Bergum Robert E - A N G - Mpls
5. Watkins - Reg - Mississippi
6. Russell Smith - Army - New Jersey
7. Gregory - Reg - Pontiac Mich
8. Flanagan - Reg - Pennsylvania

Staff Sergeant Roger Owen Paulson,
Minnesota Air National Guard, 1953-1962

Auto-Pilot Technician

Roger on a mission trip with Operation Mobilization in Israel

Roadtrip across America to meet Orinda's father, Evar Karlberg

Roger's parents, Victor and Ann Paulson

Roger with Orinda's Mom, Alta Karlberg

Last day as a single man!

Orinda (also known as Rindy) with Karen Mycue, her wonderful roommate and personal attendant for the wedding

Oh no! It's time!

Dear friends Merrill and Jan with Rindy and Roger

Dressed up for a costume party!

Roger goofing with his dad.

Roger washing dishes at cousin LaVon's house

ABOVE: Roger's heavily marked Bible

BELOW: Roger carried a smaller pocket Bible with him while at work. It, too, is covered in notes from careful study

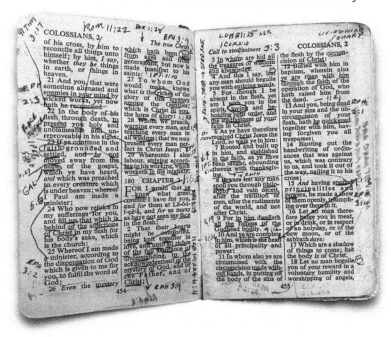

Roger worked for Handicabs. He loved his job – driving mentally handicapped adults and children to schools and daycares in the mornings and back home in the evenings. In the middle of the day, he drove veterans from the Veteran's Hospital back home to their loved ones. Weekends often found him driving veterans to their out-of-state homes.

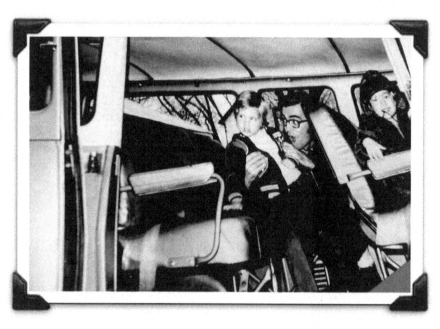

Roger displaying Handicabs birthday cake made by
his new wife!

Roger decorating a cake in the likeness of his wife. He
makes her nose HUGE! Not nice, Roger!

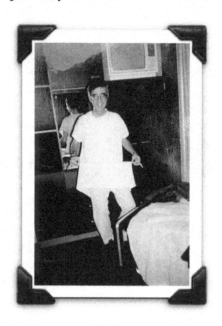

Roger before and after
Splenenectomy surgery

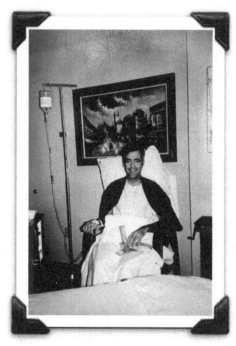

Last Christmas, 1981

Rindy swimming alone in the Radisson pool

Last anniversary - Duluth Radisson revolving restaurant

The last picture taken of Roger before tragedy struck
Roger, Rindy, and Pastor, Best Man, and Navigator mentor,
John Hartzell

Chapter 11

The Plans

After several weeks, the Lady began to question her circumstances. She was engaged with no guarantees. She should have been planning the wedding and showing off her engagement ring. But there was no ring. There was no wedding date. The wedding was not even discussed.

"Was she trapped in a very bad fairytale?" she asked herself. "Where was the happy ending?"

"How can this be, my Lord?" she asked. "Am I fooling myself? What should I do?"

And He seemed to say, "Sing the song."

So she did.

Trust in Him, ye saints, forever;

> *He is faithful, changing never;*
>
> *neither force nor guile can sever*
>
> *those He loves from Him.*

"I know, I know Lord – but it's so hard! Help me to choose to trust you even if the Prince leaves me."

And the Lord whispered into her mind again, "Keep singing."

> *Keep us, Lord, O keep us cleaving*
>
> *to Thyself and still believing,*
>
> *till the hour of our receiving*
>
> *promised joys with Thee.*

Her soul was bathed by the mental music and perfect words.

She softly spoke, "Lord, I love you! Please don't tell the Prince I am doubting him."

The next time the Lady saw the Prince, her hives were red hot and circled her entire neck like a tight red boa. Even the Prince noticed her scarlet accessory. He inquired.

"Your neck seems to have a rash. Are you all right?"

"It's just hives – I get them from time to time."

"What from?"

"Oh, if I'm worried about something or just under a little stress."

"Is there something bothering you at school?" asked the Prince, searching deep into her eyes.

"No, no," she answered (school was the only normal thing that didn't produce stress right now).

"Well, what do you think it is? Is it anything about us? We could pray about that together," he questioned as he pulled her close and looked deep into her eyes again.

"I can't tell him," she told her mind that was fighting between honesty and self-protection. But the Prince's penetrating chocolate eyes destroyed her boundary of privacy.

"I'm concerned about our future," She blurted.

"And why is that, my Lady?"

"We talk about plans but there is so much waiting. There seems to be so many dreams that are never realized."

He pulled away from her in deep thought. Time was suspended.

"Why was he so quiet? Was he waiting with a purpose?" she mused. "Was he having second thoughts? Was he only pretending to be her Prince?"

The Lady's thoughts were interrupted.

"It's time... Let's go together and see your father," announced the Prince.

"What?" retorted the Lady. "He lives in Seattle. I haven't seen him in seven years. He hardly ever sends me a birthday card. He really doesn't care."

"Well," offered the Prince, "Can you call or write?"

He could tell that the Lady needed concrete commitment.

"But it's a three-day drive. We would need a motel and my sister would be very against that situation," explained the Lady.

She was fearful about his fearless offer.

"Can we not trust our Lord to keep us pure on a journey as well in our daily lives?" questioned the Prince. "Did we not pray a commitment to our Lord together about this very thing?"

"Yes," she quietly surrendered.

"Tell me about your father," questioned the Prince.

"Well, he's 100% Swede so he does strange things like drinking his coffee out of his saucer. He loves sweets and even puts whipped cream on his pan cakes. When I was little, we saw him once a month ..." and she shared the saga of her obedient mother bringing the girls by court order to see their father at the Woodland Park Zoo.

"Daddy was fun – he danced around like a clown and taught us silly songs. When he stopped sending child support, the visits stopped and we didn't get to see him much after that. He always had a new wife and the one he has now is not friendly."

"As one thoroughbred Swede to another, I am looking forward to meeting your father," announced the Prince, adding, "And what about your Mother?"

"She lives in North Platte, Nebraska and writes me often. She would love to meet you."

"Well, let's not disappoint her," he cheerfully offered. "In this circumstance, we should ask her as well."

So began the plans to drive miles and miles to Nebraska and then over and through the mountains of Montana and Idaho to Washington State. When the Lady shared their plans with her married sister, she was greatly vexed by a young couple driving on a long trip when they were only engaged. But the Lady and her Prince had the peace of approval from their Lord. They found great amusement asking at the motel check-in desks for two rooms. It did puzzle many. Sometimes, it opened up conversations with strangers about their faith.

Travel provided an abundant amount of time to talk about future plans, likes and dislikes, growing-up memories, and dreams. The evenings found them in God's Word together. The Prince had suggested that they study the book of Nehemiah. It seemed like a strange book but as the couple dug into the details of the man, Nehemiah, and his focus to rebuild the damaged wall for his beloved city, the Lady became attached to the story. So much so, that she paralleled the events of Nehemiah to her relationship with the Prince.

In the month of Chislev (November/December) the man, Nehemiah, heard that the wall of his beloved city was destroyed and the gates were burned with fire. December 1 was the Prince and the Lady's first date.

Nehemiah pleaded in prayer to the Lord for favor from the King Artaxerxes. He took the risk to bare his heart and share his requests. Nehemiah served the king as a wine taster. He was never allowed to show sadness nor personal distress. The Lady could surely relate to the stress of trying to hide her feelings about the unknown.

Nehemiah is granted his request and takes action in the month of Nisan. The Prince proposed in March and that would be Nehemiah's month of Nisan.

Rebuilding the wall began and 52 days later the wall was finished. The commitment of engagement for the Prince and the Lady began March 17 and 52 days later the first action, the cross-country trip, was building the scaffolding toward the approaching marriage.

The building of the wall correlated with the laminating of their relationship. They were now on their way to meet her mother and father for the blessing to marry.

As they rumbled down the dirt roads in North Platte, the Lady tried her best to remember the way to the little flat that her mother shared with her brother. Sure enough, the red horse icon of the old gas station was still there. After a few jogs in the road, there was her mother, seated in a lawn chair waiting for them. She leaped up like a little plump fairy godmother ready to use her magic wand for something wonderful. The Prince helped the Lady out of the car just as her Mom arrived with arms open wide.

"Mom," the Lady shouted.

The two women embraced with hugs and kisses.

"How are you, honey?" her Mom asked. "I'm so glad you came. And is this your Prince?"

"Yes, he is," admitted the Lady with a blush that revealed her private confidant.

"Hello, Roger. I've heard many things about you. Pages to be exact."

"Mom, shhh. Don't tell everything."

"Well," offered Sir Roger, "Everything that is good could be true and everything that is not good we could talk about."

As they all laughed, her mother showed them into the little flat. Dreams and plans were shared over coffee cake and hot java.

The next morning the couple left with joy in their hearts and the blessings from her mother.

The second part of their traveling adventure provided affirmations of their Lord's presence. Mountain roads were scenic and shouted of God's glorious creation, but they were also narrow and full of curves. Beginning the trek over the Big Horn Mountains in the late afternoon was not a great decision – even if the motel was holding their reservation for late arrival. Since mountain roads have no electric lights, only the lightening revealed the abyss on the passenger's side. The sharp curves that the headlights illuminated made her gasp and hold her breath. A loud boom announced the flash of bright, ugly fingers of electricity that seemed to try to grab the car. The Prince would calmly announce "Someone in Heaven wants another picture. Smile!"

In the wee hours of the morning, they arrived at the tiny motel in Cody, Wyoming. The faithful motel clerk had saved their reservation and the couple staggered to their rooms with thankful hearts and weary minds.

Other events that showed them the Lord's abiding presence, included their car surprises. One day, the muffler blew and the noise was not only an attention getter but also very annoying. Finding a repair garage on a Sunday was not hard for the Lord. They were delayed a few hours and thankfully gave only $6.00 for the help. Another time, the gas attendant found the fan belt so thin it was about to bust. Again, the couple thanked the Lord for His protection.

It seemed too soon to arrive in Seattle. The Lady was delighted to introduce Sir Roger to the Ocean, Mt. Rainier, Hick's Lake, the Space Needle, her humble house, blackberry bushes, and her father.

Daddy was filled with joy at the Prince's request. He literally placed the Lady's hand into the Prince's and pressed them together. He even cried a tear and exclaimed, "I truly feel like a father!"

The couple felt blessed and the trip home propelled them into definite action. Yes, they sang and sang and continued to study Nehemiah together. Like the dedication of Nehemiah's wall, detailed plans were made and the date was set for the ceremony.

Peace anointed the Lady's heart.

Chapter 12

The Dedication

Alone in the bridal dressing room, the Lady waited with anticipation, occupying her mind by practicing the written vows she had created especially for her Prince. Her thoughts jumped to the intriguing story of Nehemiah and how it paralleled the relationship of Sir Roger and herself from start to finish.

Nehemiah, the man, first learns of the demolished condition of the wall around his beloved Jerusalem in the Jewish month of Chislev (November/December). The Prince and the Lady encounter each other in November; their first date is December 1st.

In the month of Nisan (March/April), Nehemiah, with permission, begins rebuilding the broken wall.

March 17th the Prince proposes and the Lady accepts.

In the Jewish month of Elul (August/September), the wall was finished. It took 52 days. The Lady had actually counted the days from the proposal to the first step of action – the trip cross country to see her parents – and that was exactly 52 days.

And now, in the Jewish month of Tishri (September/October) Nehemiah orchestrated the dedication of the finished wall. The Prince and the Lady were embarking on their October 12th dedication of their lives being laminated together in marriage.

"So like our journey," thought the Lady, "The highlights of our relationship and wedding dedication details so parallel the story of Nehemiah like it was all pre-planned by YOU, Lord."

Together they had selected the music, musicians, vocalists, scripture readings, and Pastor Unruh. Everything was perfect. Even the lemon meringue ice cream and the three-layered cake with white, lacy icing that draped down over the edges – suspended in air.

"I wish the real Nehemiah could be one of our guests," the Bride spoke softly to herself.

Reality returned when Karen Mycue, her personal attendant, slipped back into the room.

"The prelude has begun and little Lynette has professionally lit all of the candelabrums. I can't believe she is only 8 years old. The bridesmaids are lined up waiting for their cue to walk the isle. And, the groomsmen have entered the side door with *YOUR HANDSOME PRINCE*. The men look a little anxious. But, Roger looks like a confident, royal Prince," she gleefully blurted.

The three-layered cake with white, lacy icing that draped down over the edges – suspended in air.

"He is," the Lady added.

With that, Karen Mycue swept up the billows of yardage that extended from the back of the bridal gown and the two of them floated together out of the Bride's dressing room into the church foyer. The beautiful solo voice of Karen Buckholtz announced the sacredness of the Dedication:

There's a sweet, sweet spirit in this place,

And I know it is the Spirit of the Lord;

The Bride cradled every word in her heart.

"So perfect," she mused.

The organ, under the gifted hands of Jack Simon, softly began *Jesu, Joy of Man's Desiring*. On cue, each bridesmaids began her slow walk down the aisle in a melodic procession.

From Left to Right: *Jolene, Lynette, and Mynda, who called Roger her "Uncle Froger."*

Jolene, her youngest niece, looked like a young maiden instead of an 11 year-old child. Her floor length sage-green gown highlighted the basket of yellow fall flowers that she carried. Next, JoAnn Innes, her dear teaching friend, followed by Jan Olson, A true soul mate. Last, her sister Ilene – regal and truly the Maid of Honor. Each bridesmaid wore the same floor length sage-green gown and carried a basket of yellow fall flowers. Her sister had made every gown, not to mention the Bride's gown and their mother's frock. The Lady was basking in the love that was represented in the beauty of all the elegant wedding attire.

When everyone was in place, little 5 year-old Mynda slowly walked down the aisle in her mini sage-green floor length gown and dropped yellow rose petals from her basket. Those precious yellow petals were given to the Lady by The Prince and had been saved over the months for this moment. Little Mynda must had realized how precious they were as you only dropped three petals during her long, slow stroll to the altar.

The trumpet gave a piercing announcement that the Bride was coming. The Lady gently tucked her arm under her waiting brother-in-law's elbow and said, "Take your time, John, I want to enjoy every minute."

John, Orinda's brother-in-law, walking her down the aisle

She glowed with happiness – nothing sad could penetrate the blessed harmony of the moment. A fleeting thought attacked her joy, "I wish Daddy could be the one to give me away. I wish he could just be here. Oh well," she dismissed the sadness, "at least he gave us his permission and his blessing. And, I know I have My Lord's blessing. He has provided my brother-in-law to give me away in my father's place! How fitting, John really has been like a father to me – a counselor, encourager, dependable pillar for my crazy problems. Now the Prince will take his place."

Again, she felt blessed. She felt loved.

She glanced at John. How full of joy he was for her.

"I feel such peace," she mused underneath her smiles of greeting.

The aisle seemed a mile long – bordered with joyous friends and family. She could see the Prince at the end of her journey – waiting – just like he had done for months, yes, years – waiting for the Lord to show him who to woo and court and when to propose.

The Lord truly did know her inner most needs as the Prince was so much more than she could ever think to request of her Lord. And she felt the Lord's love engulf her when she was in the Prince's presence. His proud glow and wide smile of approval as she glided toward him made her heart beat with anticipation. He gazed at her in awe, like she was a treasured Dresden doll. And she loved it.

Orinda's sister spent weeks making all the dresses, but the most elegant was the wedding gown.

She was wearing LOVE. Her sister spent weeks making all the dresses, but the most magnificent was the wedding gown. The white opaque material that overlayed the satin foundation was actually called "sheer delight." Flowing from her waist like a waterfall, her princess shoes peeked out with each step. Delicate lace encased her bodice, revealing just enough of her youthful breasts to announce that she was a woman. Puffs of "sheer delight" bloomed from the lace shoulder caps and flowed to her lace wristlets. A white tulle veil cascaded over her face from a wreath of white satin leaves. (Her sister had worn that same wreath when she married John. That was tradition – wearing something borrowed.) Bursting from under a huge satin bow in the small of her back, the train cascaded down to the floor spreading out over the whole aisle like the tail feathers of a peacock. The train made her feel like a Princess Bride – and that was exactly what she was – the Lord's Princess.

Down the aisle, about a mile away, was her handsome Prince. And he was gorgeous. His lemon tuxedo with the black velvet piping and black velvet bowtie enhanced his ebony hair. He stood erect like a toy soldier. The satin strip on his sleek black pants dropped down to his shiny shoes. They glistened in the sun light that pierced its presence through the stained glass cross in the window behind his back. The black cummerbund. The white ruffled shirt. The Prince was perfect.

As the Bride approached the Prince, he stepped forward to receive her. She felt like Cinderella being delivered by an entourage into the keeping of her secret lover.

She whispered softly, "How are you doing?" As she had heard that a marriage ceremony was stressful on men and some had even fainted.

"Great," replied the Prince. And his confidence gave her peace.

Chimes rang as they stepped up onto the altar to dedicate themselves to each other. The soloist, Karen B., began her musical announcement accompanied by JoAnn on the guitar, *There Is Love.*

Her mind flipped to the vows. She hoped she could remember them as she and the Prince had individually written their own vows. They wished to communicate their commitment to each other and their gratefulness to the Lord for bringing them together.

The Prince spoke first. It really was a prayer of thanksgiving and promise to the Lady and the Lord. He held her hands – drowning them in his loving hands and began to pray. It was so soft, so pure, so private.

"Heavenly Father, thank you for this 'gift' that you have given me – the inheritance that I have looked forward to for many years."

Then opening his eyes – he gazed into hers and said:

"Orinda, I love you and I receive you as my Bride. I pray that I might be that example as Christ was to the church – to love you, to cherish you, to look after your physical needs – to make those things real to you even as Christ has made them real to the Church. Orinda, at that time when Christ receives you unto himself, I pray that you might stand without shame and that we might all rejoice together at that time when He comes back."

The Lady melted in his gaze and almost forgot her carefully practiced words.

"Roger, I love you and I believe that God has brought us together and provided you as my husband and my spiritual leader. I accept you as a Love Gift from God. With Christ as my strength, I will help you, obey you, and follow you throughout all the circumstances that God leads us through until He separates us by death."

They exchanged their rings as symbols of their Lord's eternal love for each of them and for their vow of commitment and faithfulness till death separated them. Each held a candle and together lit the Unity candle as the guitar joined the organ in *The New 23rd Psalm*. JoAnn and Karen B. sang it together.

The Pastor's blessing was so eloquent.

"Thank you for Roger and Orinda and the wonderful way they have experienced the reality of Jesus Christ in their lives and now the way in which you have brought them together to form a union in HIM. May they know YOUR strength and YOUR comfort. To the human joys may be added the dimension of joy unspeakable as everything shared together be shared with Christ their Lord and Savior. May the difficult tasks that pass their paths in life be seen relatively easy to bear because they have each other. May your PEACE and our JOY be theirs. So affirm this relationship, convince them so thoroughly that this union was designed in Heaven. And Lord, do it by your abundant blessings – so manifold that even as they share them with us, they will not lack the ability to express the great things that God has done and is doing for them."

"What now God hath joined together, let not man put asunder."

-Mark 10:9

"In as much as Roger Owen Paulson and Orinda Ardith Karlberg have consented together in holy wedlock and have witnessed the same before God and this company – by the authority committed unto me as a minister of the church of Jesus Christ – I now pronounce you Husband and Wife."

At this point, the Prince carefully lifted the Princess's veil and kissed his Bride. The seal of heaven was stamped on her lips – forever. The music burst with triumph and applause exploded as they turned to face "their Court." The booming voice of

Pastor Unruh quieted the guests with his final prayer.

"Let us pray."

"May the Lord bless you and keep you in your rising up and lying down, in your coming in and going out, in your labor and in your leisure, in your laughter and in your tears, until you come to stand before HIM in that great day where there is no sunset and no dawn – Amen."

"May I present to you – Mr. and Mrs. Roger Paulson."

As the congregation clapped, the couple floated down the aisle, arm-in-arm, aglow with love complete!

And the Lord blessed the marriage dedication. He beamed his glory through the stain glass cross embedded in the sanctuary window and the prisms of light shone on the man and his wife.

The Prince and his Lady:
Mr. & Mrs. Roger Paulson
October 12, 1974

"... And the Lord blessed the marriage dedication. He beamed his glory through the stain glass cross embedded in the sanctuary window and the prisms of light shone on the man and his wife."

"Live joyfully with the wife whom thou lovest all the days of the life of thy vanity which He hath given thee under the sun."
- Ecclesiastes 9:9

"When a man hath taken a new wife, he shall not go out to war, neither shall he be charged with any business, but he shall be free at home one year and shall cheer up his wife whom he hath taken."
-Deuteronomy 24.5

Chapter 13

The Focus

The Prince always took the Lord's words to heart and so it was reflected in their first year of marriage. He excused himself from all commitments to be home with his Bride. He sold the TV and any other distractions in order to lavish his attention on her. She loved it and was always bubbling with joy.

The Bride began to develop her housekeeping skills in the manner that pleased her Prince. They grew to love and respect each other and delight in each new thing that came their way. Everything was a duet, from laundry to grocery shopping.

Friday nights, they would tumble into the car and go to the Red Owl grocery store. The Bride had the list and the Prince had the coupons. They would literally waltz up and down the isles picking out an item right on the beat of the store's background music. Sometimes he would push the grocery cart with her clinging to the frame on the front end. Or he would grab her and swing her into a twirl. One time he scooped her up and she let out a squeal of delight of which brought an employee to investigate.

"Is everything all right?" he blurted.

"Everything is just perfect," announced the Prince with a wink of admiration sent silently to his wife.

They had each other and there was JOY! The Lord's JOY!

The Lady felt complete – total wholeness enveloped her being. She glowed from his loving favor and encouragement and she felt strong and vibrant – able to risk being her total self.

In such a loving accepting environment, her weaknesses seemed easy to overcome. In fact, the

Prince and the Lady made a little game that surfaced some of their pseudo insecurities. It went like this:

"I'll tell you 3 things I like about you and you do the same for me," chirped the Bride. "Then, you tell me something I need to change and I will do the same for you."

They became a mirror for each other, reflecting and magnifying character strengths and revealing and drawing out the flaws. Even friends and family noticed.

"Have you noticed how Sir Roger is more out going, more self-assured," they commented. "And the Lady – much calmer, stable, and deeper. They certainly do bring out the best in each other. Their joy radiates the whole room when they enter. Their marriage is like a Fairytale made in Heaven."

It was evident that day after day their lives were being laminated in love.

"Two truly do become one in marriage," commented the Prince. "You are more precious to me than my own life."

Life was beautiful – so happy, so exciting. Even their arguments brought sweet reconciliation.

"What? We can't get another car until we have ALL the money? That's thousands of dollars. It will take years."

"Well," began the Prince slowly, " As your appointed 'Bishop,' I want to seriously live up to my spiritual role. Let's pray about it together, get into the Lord's WORD, and then we can discuss it."

She agreed.

Sure enough, there was scripture in God's Word that talked about wisdom in purchases and being a good steward of their monies and belongings. So, the Bride learned the pattern – pray together, go to God's Word, and discuss the issue together. And as they were focusing on each other that first year, they were also learning to focus together on their Lord.

Chapter 14

The Compromise

*D*ays turned into weeks, weeks to months, and months to years. Each new year was better than the last. The Prince and his wife became laminated as best friends, intimate lovers, dependable helpmates, confidential confidants, and uplifting encouragers. Their disagreements were sweet, gentle, and direct – their affirmations, sincere. Their relationship touched other lives around them and spread such joy. The Lady was so grateful to her Lord for giving her this beautiful "gift" of His love in the Prince. And, Sir Roger was beaming with the abundance of a life truly blessed by tis Lord.

The Prince took his spiritual role seriously. He spent much time praying with his Lady and listening – helping her find answers to life in the Bible. Daily, the Prince spent many minutes in private study and conversation with their Lord. The pages of his Holy Bible were yellowed on the outer edges as well as underlined, cross referenced, and decorated with personal notes. Sir Roger drank deeply from the well of knowledge in the Lord's words. His relationship with his Lord was intimate and active.

Each morning he arose before dawn and kneeled by the bed while the Lady still slumbered. There he talked with their Lord in prayer – lifting up the cares of friends and family. After breakfast, which he ate with the Lord because his wife still slept, he packed up his Bible and the creative lunch that the Lady had packed for him the night before. Both were deposited into his empty grocery bag as he slipped into his Handicab jacket. Then he crept up the stairs to place a kiss on his "Sleeping Beauty." She would return his sweet affection and bid him "Goodbye, love" before she re-entered slumber.

In the evening, the Prince would race home and bound in the front door. He would wrap his arms around his little wife and plant a big kiss on her lips.

"I thought of you today," he would open. "I had my delicious lunch at the city park across the street from Eitel Hospital. As I was sitting on the bench reading my Bible, *AND*, enjoying that peanut butter and dill pickle sandwich, a little bird sat right by my head on an overhanging branch. I could barely see him for the blossoms were so thick. He began to sing and it was then I wished you could have been there to share it with me. The sun was bright and warm, the air was fragrant with spring, and I was filled with thankfulness. I thanked the Lord again for you. You are precious to me!"

And he planted a kiss on her forehead.

"And, how was your day?"

"Wonderful. I wished you were there with me playing tag with my first graders. You are so good with children. I wish we had a little one ourselves."

"In His time, my dear," offered the Prince.

"Well, you were on my mind as well," interjected the Lady. "It was such a lovely day. When the children began to play with each other, it gave me a little break. I paused to notice the clear azure sky. It reminded me of last week when we flew our kite. Remember how high we got it. Wow! Three rolls of string before it broke. Too bad we couldn't find it. Maybe it's in Africa?"

"You are such a kid. We don't need a child," he laughed. "I love you!"

On and on they spilled out their day's events, delighting in each other's company. So glad were they to be together again – until after they finished the dishes. Then the Prince would retreat into the Aunt Disa room (the guest room named for the Lady's Swedish Aunt) with only the Lord and His Holy

Book. He would spend an hour or more searching, studying, musing, meditating, and praying. It became a problem their first year of marriage. The Lady would busy herself with sewing or cleaning or preparations for the next school day, but she was lonely and fearful that a wedge was developing in their relationship.

She often thought, "Was she selfish to expect his attention so much? Why wasn't she happy that he was growing closer and closer to the Lord? Wasn't their Lord the ultimate source of their JOY? The whole reason they were together?"

She finally decided to intrude on his privacy and present her wounded, fearful thoughts. But, inside she was afraid he would spurn her for her lack of interest in the Lord's precepts. She would take the risk.

She quietly walked up the stairs, spreading a path of prayer before her. She timidly knocked on the door. *Tap, tap.*

"What is it, my love?" came the invitation.

She opened the door to see a sea of open books and scattered papers surrounding him like a moat around a castle. He sat in a Buddha position, pen in one hand and his Bible in the other. The notebook on his lap was filled with color coded notes and margin references.

"What are you doing?" she inquired while eyeing all the paraphernalia.

"Oh, just studying." responded the Prince. "Look at this!" he spoke out excitedly.

And he would share with her his latest insights into the deep, deep depths of their Lord's Holy Book.

"You love studying, don't you?" she questioned.

"Oh yes, I do!" he emphatically replied. "It's my life and, next to you it's the most important part of my life."

"So, this is different than our time together praying and reading the Bible?" She asked.

"Oh yes," he softly shared, "This is when our Lord gives me guidance on how to be a better husband for you and a faithful servant for HIM. But, tell me what is on your heart?"

"Oh, I was just feeling lonely." There, she said it.

"I mean, you're up here so long at a time. I guess I just miss you even though you are right upstairs. Sometimes, I feel jealous of our Lord. I know I shouldn't, but HE already knows my heart."

She lowered her eyes and waited for his reply.

The Prince grabbed her hands and pulled her close to him – wrapping her up with his warm loving arms.

"Maybe, we can do some deep study together if you would like. I am so sorry I've been selfish. You can join me anytime and I will even set a timer so I remember to take a break with you."

"Thanks, love," she softly spoke as she soaked up his chocolate eyes of affection.

As she got up to leave, she felt very close to the Lord. It was good.

"I love you very much," she said, as she slowly shut the door.

"Oh Lord," she mused, "who could not love and respect such a sensitive, thoughtful man as this? Thank you, Lord, for such a beautiful 'Love Gift'!"

Chapter 15

The Anniversary

The Prince had decided to take his Lady on a mystery road trip to celebrate their anniversary. Seven years had flown by like Cinderella's evening ball.

"Give me a hint of our destination," she chided as she closed their suitcase and followed the Prince to the car.

"What a perfect day!" the Price announced. "Just look at all the colors of the trees against the azure blue sky. Isn't God creative? It's just like the Indian Summer day we were married. I planned it this way," he announced with a chuckle as he closed the trunk.

"Are we going up North to look at the leaves? asked the Lady.

"We are going to see an abundance of color," the Prince responded.

He started the car and they backed out of the garage and started up the hill to the highway.

"Are we going north or south?" she asked.

"Well, first we go south, then we go west, then north and finally a little east," he teased.

"Red Wing?" she offered.

"No, no, too far south." answered the Prince.

"Stillwater?" she rebounded.

"No, much farther north," he responded.

"Duluth?" she asked.

"Yes," he gleefully replied with a nod.

"Duluth!" she repeated. "Oh, how perfect!" she spilled out with joy.

"Where are we staying?" she asked

"I can't tell you everything!" he chided.

And they settled in for the three hour drive.

The scenery was breath-taking and they both were awed by the beauty of the colorful leaves waving their red, yellow and orange fingers of welcome. As they breezed by on the tree-lined highway, they felt like they had entered an autumn painting.

Their minds were busy day dreaming of expectations and unrest. They didn't talk much, nor did they sing. A somber spirit of concern had invaded their autumn world.

"Do you think this trip will cause your legs to hurt?" she asked the Prince.

"No, I didn't have any pink dots the last two days," he responded.

"I wish we would have known *NOT* to rub down your legs with liniment," she softly offered.

"Well, we didn't know, and anyway this upcoming surgery is supposed to fix everything. Remember there's an 85% chance it will do the trick and that's a high percentage. We will trust our Lord," he stated. "So, no more fuss about it. This weekend is for you and I to be together and that's our focus," the Prince declared.

As they drew near Duluth, they began to see the shipping cranes, grain loaders, railroad tracks, and bridges. Lake Superior seemed all dressed up in sparkling glitter as a welcome gesture to them. The azure blue sky, the sparkling lake girded with gorgeous colorful trees. They stopped at a look out to just drink it into their souls.

"God is so creative. It's beautiful!" commented the Prince.

"Yes, this is certainly going to be a special weekend. Maybe the best anniversary we have had yet," offered the Lady.

They arrived at the Duluth Radisson Hotel, checked in, and found their room. The Prince set down the luggage and unlocked the door.

"May I," he said with a bow.

"Of course," replied the Lady as he swooped her up into his arms and stepped across the threshold.

She laughed with glee, partly at the fond memories of days gone by, and partly to cover up the gnawing realization that the Prince was not quite as strong and steady. She quickly became animated with the excitement of staying at a very fancy hotel. She had overheard the hotel clerk verify their 5:00PM reservation for dining in the revolving restaurant on the 18th floor. It was so perfect.

She twirled around the room, arms flailing as she leaped and landed lightly like Tinker Bell. And then she stopped.

"Roger, can we afford this?" she inquired with a serious tone.

The Radisson Hotel in Duluth, Minnesota

"Well," responded the Prince, "I have had a few squirrels burying our funds for several months.

Sometimes, a special weekend is more important than putting extra money aside for possible medical expenses. And, besides, the squirrels were looking for a job."

"Just look at the view," the Lady commented, changing the subject. "The lake goes on forever. Beautiful!"

The Prince came to her side and together they awed the beauty of Lake Superior and the autumn nature huddling among the stately buildings of Duluth.

"This, truly is a picture window!" exclaimed the Prince. "Get the camera, Honey, and let's snap this as a permanent souvenir."

She obeyed quickly and returned with a piece of luggage and plopped it on and bed and began to rummage for the camera.

"Did you notice that we have two beds?" She pointed out.

"Well, let's use one for luggage and the other for us. We won't need all of one bed the way you push me onto the edge," he teased.

"You're right", she laughed, anticipating their nightly ritual.

They would lie side by side holding hands and talk out loud to their Lord. Then, the Prince would draw her close to him and kiss her gently.

"Good night, my darling, I love you."

And she would respond, "Good night, my love."

And they would drift off to sleep in each other's arms.

"Let's go for a swim in that pool," she announced, as she whipped out their bathing suits.

That was part of the plans.

As they were undressing to swim, the Prince noticed some small red eruptions girding his lower torso.

"What is this?" questioned the Prince. "They burn a little."

"And they are too big to be petechiae," offered the Lady. "Unless, this just looks different because its not the capillaries in the leg area that are bleeding. Maybe we shouldn't swim."

"No, no," he retorted. You swim and enjoy. I will sit by the pool and be your life guard. I have red lifeguard trunks, and a book, of course."

"Well, all right. I won't swim long," she answered.

So, the Lady splashed and floated and dolphin-dived for a short time. It wasn't fun to swim alone and she was concerned about this new arrival of another medical mystery. Her mind constantly meandered down the dark path that she did not really want to entertain. This new rash just did not fit in with their anniversary plans. They had been battling this disease for two years now. It had been an uphill battle with little hope as the disease was not responding to the strong doses of steroids.

Surgery to remove the spleen was scheduled and their hopes were high that this would stop the killer lurking in his bone marrow. Platelets clot the blood, and every platelet created in his bone marrow was viciously killed by his confused antibodies. That's how auto immune diseases work. Your body tries to kill your body.

Easy bleeding was always a problem. In fact, that is how the disease was first discovered. The Prince was bleeding from an area where men do not bleed. When he sought medical help, they put him on heavy does of antibiotics, announcing it as a bladder infection. A few months later, they discovered bruise marks on his arms and body and red speckled petechiae on his legs. These little red dots were really bleeding capillaries.

After a 10-12 hour driving day, his legs would ache and she would rub them with old fashion liniment to relieve the pain. Not knowing that the rash was a signal of something serious and the very ingredients in the liniment was actually causing more damage, they continued this medicine cabinet therapy until they found out the truth. What a devastating blow to both of them! The doctors put him on a steroid call prednisone. It bloated his body, gave him a moon face and ate his stomach lining which resulted many times in horrid breath. Yet, she loved him fiercely and tried ever so hard to trust their Lord.

"Lord," she cried in her mind, "I feel a nagging fear inside me. Help me to trust YOU! I know that you won't allow anything to happen to us that hasn't passed before you for permission. Somehow, I will trust you and not lean on my own understanding." (Proverbs 3:5)

She had reached the perch where the Prince was deeply engaged in the pages of a book. She bent over to give him a kiss. As he lifted his head toward her, she violently shook her dripping locks of hair and giggled with glee.

"Hey, my book," he announced as he pulled her close into the chair with him to collect the kiss she teasingly offered.

"Oh, who cares about your ol' book. You like books more than me," she taunted.

"That's not true," he softly exclaimed as he kissed her again on the forehead. "You are more precious to me than anything in this world."

"I know," she quietly responded with a hidden concern at how quickly he went from giddy to serious these days.

"You are my precious 'love gift' from our Lord," she confessed. "I love you so very much!"

And they sealed their confessions with a passionate kiss.

They talked for several minutes, reminiscing about past anniversaries and reliving the celebrations of their love for each other. They were so laminated in their marriage.

Underneath, the Lady was trying to avoid asking about the new rash – the Invader. Finally, the anxiety of the unknown forced her to inquire, "Say, let's look at that rash."

As she lifted his shirt she could hardly keep from gasping. There was a marked change. The rash had become prominent in a pathway on each side of his abdomen from his back to above his navel. Each little tiny point was about twice the original size and seemed to be like a blister. The Lady tried to keep her voice calm and panic out of her stomach.

"We need to call the doctor," said the Lady and collected their things.

"Well," said the Prince, trying to be light hearted, "At least they are organized – right in a row on both sides."

As soon as they reached their room, the Prince made a bee line for the phone.

The doctor told him to show up anytime tomorrow as soon as they had reached town. The Prince put the phone down and sadly said, "This changes things. I'm sorry, Love, we must return tomorrow. But, let's still keep our dinner reservations and enjoy the rest of the evening. God knows all about this. We can trust HIM."

"I know," the Lady agreed solemnly.

Dinner was lovely but very quiet. The Prince was a little embarrassed that he couldn't shave. Even a nick could start a bleed. The Lady tried to console him with the fact that there were dim lights in the restaurant and every man looked like he had a 5 o'clock shadow.

"After all," she said, "It *IS* 5:00PM."

Decisions were made to pack to up and leave at day break. They were united in the focus to get to Dr. Levitan as quickly as possible because the spleen surgery – their only hope – was less than a week away.

"I think we should each take a bed tonight," the Prince announced. "I don't want to disturb you if I need to get up, and I want to be careful with this little red army."

"Yes, good idea," agreed the Lady but inside she desperately needed their nightly ritual – especially this very night.

"Perhaps that's why the Lord provided us with two beds," she offered.

Morning came quickly even though neither slept. The Prince was in constant burning pain and the Lady was battling fear. They both had their own giants to conquer. They prayed together, loaded the car, and drove back to the Twin Cities. Very few words were spoken. They tried to sing, but it was too hard.

"How could this wicked Invader show up on their anniversary?"

She was heart sick and very scared.

Neither one knew how they got to Dr. Levitan's office. It was automatic. The doctor escorted Roger into the exam room and came back for the Lady immediately.

"This is very serious," Dr. Levitan said. "It is right on the surgery line. We cannot do surgery till this is healed."

So, shingles, this unwanted anniversary gift, aborted the surgery.

Chapter 16

The Waiting Room

Since the diagnosis of Idiopathic Thrombocytopenia, (ITP), the Prince and his Beloved seemed to be in constant battles with unsurmountable life issues.

It seemed like a huge fire-raging dragon was tracking them down and constantly breathing out blasts of pain, fear, and hopelessness. The Prince kept his shield of faith and the Sword of the Spirit (his Bible) on his night stand. The Lady bathed herself in prayer and scripture that she had memorized. ITP was lurking around every corner of their lives and had now snuck onto the scene of a severe case of Shingles. This dragon was bloody, painful, and unrelenting. The row of blisters that Shingles had created were now filled with blood and were very painful. The Lady would dab them with

Calamine Lotion and hot packs trying to give the Prince some relief. One bright red, bloody blister about the size of a bottle cap, hung down like a half-filled balloon. But the Prince fought the pain bravely and she stayed by his side.

Other unsurmountable giants joined the battle. His platelet count was in the danger zone (below 20,000). This caused spontaneous bleeding – filling the blisters – and easy bruising anywhere on the body. The platelets, which clot the blood, were being attacked as soon as they were created and immediately destroyed right within his bone marrow. ITP was trying to take his life. It was almost too much to bear.

Since the Prince was too sick to go to work, he had no income. He loved his job with Handicabs – driving mentally handicapped adults and children to schools and day cares in the mornings and back home in the evenings. In the middle of the day, he drove veterans from the Vets Hospital back home to their loved ones. Weekends, often found him driving vets to their out-of-state homes. They loved him because he was so loving and gentle. The hours there were long, but there were no financial or medical benefits from Handicabs.

The Lady had giants to fight as well. Her school district went on strike. Teachers were expected to picket, babysit, and pass out informational flyers to the parents. She had to get someone to be with the

Prince while she was gone. To add more to the sad and heavy experience, her paycheck was frozen. But, the Prince kept their morale uplifted by constantly bringing their focus to their Lord and His Word.

"Just watch and wait for the Lord to act," the Prince would remind his Beloved, "we will trust HIM! We are in His waiting room."

A check arrived in the mail from the Chudek's, a church couple. That $100 finished paying for the October mortgage and even left $0.49 in the checking account. Many times, the Lady discovered cash in her dress coat pockets when she returned from church. Other little surprise discoveries of money which were hoarded by the "Roger Squirrels" were found and joyfully deposited into the bank.

Through it all, the Prince remained positive and faithful with such a beautiful attitude and deep trust.

Their church family and friends called regularly, sent such endearing notes, and prayed regularly. Most of them were from their long-term Bible Study group called, "The Agape Group." They truly had agape love for the Prince and the Lady. Dr. Carl Christenson, warmly known at church as "The Rear Admiral" for his career choice, was their church shepherd. He called many nights checking on the progress of the fever and blisters and then unofficially shared the updates with the other doctors that were involved. There were many people waiting for the upcoming savior – a splenectomy.

Finally, the day came. The Prince's fever broke and the blisters were slowly drying up. The surgery was scheduled and they were on a fast path to hope and health. The drive to the hospital was filled with expectations of joy and victory. However, the victory became guarded as they met with the surgeon, Dr. Betalden. In the pre-operating room, while the Prince lay on the hospital gurney, the skilled surgeon explained that Roger's platelets were still very low and if spontaneous medical bleeding occurred, there was nothing they could do. Extra blood was ready for the blood transfusions.

The couple considered the risks and agreed to go ahead with the surgery. Actually, there was no other option.

They kissed a quick "good-bye." Their eyes locked and the Prince was rolled away through the double doors of surgery. The Lady was escorted to the surgery waiting room.

There she was, all alone in His Waiting Room.

Chapter 17

The Phone Call

Time had passed. The October splenectomy was not a definite victory. His platelet count went up and down like an elevator. Many doctor visits tried to engage medicine to re-engineer his body and allow platelets to survive. The polarized feelings of joy and peace and then suddenly, fear and hope frazzled the emotions of the couple. Somehow, they lived each day knowing that their Lord was in control – even when the horizon was dark.

It was January 28th. The Lady was dressing for parent-teacher conferences with the parents of her students. She had picked out an outfit she felt that was comfortable and professional. She took extra time on her make-up. As she was brushing her hair, she heard the Prince on the phone in bathroom.

"Ed, this is Roger, I am not feeling well, and I just cannot come in today. I'm so sorry."

The phone dropped into the cradle which caused the Lady to investigate. She found the Prince sitting on the toilet with his face in his hands.

"Roger, what is it? Where do you feel bad?"

"My head, my head, it hurts so badly!"

"We are going to Unity Hospital. Remember, Dr. Christenson said if anything happens, go there first. I will call my principal after I get you to Unity."

The Prince was limp now and not very coherent. The Lady tried to lift him off the seat to get him dressed and down the stairs into the car. He was too big and very, very heavy. She just couldn't lift him off the seat.

"I'll be right back," she called as she dashed down the stairs and out the door to get help.

The neighbor came back with her – sleepy eyed and unaware of what he was getting himself into. He pulled up the Prince's pants like he was dressing a doll and somehow the two of them got the Prince down the stairs and into the car. She backed out of the garage barely missing the door scraping on the hood of the car and dashed to the hospital. As they were driving in and out of lanes to pass slow movers the Prince kept talking about cupcakes. The Lady was scared and fighting hard to stay focused.

When they arrived, she parked right at the entrance doors and dashed in to get help. Two nurses quickly came with a wheelchair and pulled his legs out of the vehicle and lifted him under his arms and knees right into the wheelchair. Then they took off like a fire engine, calling, "You can check him in at the desk!"

The Lady somehow, without knowing what she was doing, found a parking place and ran into the hospital. She was ushered immediately into a cubical and began answering questions that the admitting assistant was firing at her. She could hardly get a clear head to know all the information that they needed.

"What a blessing that his surgery information from the October splenectomy was already in the hospital records," she noted.

"Thank you, Lord," she prayed silently.

Then she remembered her first conference was in 45 minutes. She asked to use the phone.

She knew, her principal, Dr. Switzer would be at school this early.

"Dr. Switzer, this is Rindy Paulson. I am at Unity Hospital with Roger. I brought him in with a headache and he is not coherent. I will be late."

"You stay with your husband," Dr. Switzer said, "I will cancel all your conferences for today. Keep me posted and take care of Roger."

"Bless him," the Lady softly told her Lord.

A nurse appeared and inquired, "Are you Mrs. Paulson?"

"Yes," responded the Lady

"Follow me. I will take you to him. He is in the ICU (Intensive Care Unit)," she announced.

The Lady followed her into a white room with lots of lights. Movable curtains wrapped around the beds making little private spaces. The nurse pulled the curtain aside and there was the Prince. She was so shocked she could hardly stay standing.

"What is happening?" she asked the nurse and the ICU doctor hovering over the thrashing body.

They acknowledged her presence and made a path for her to approach the Prince. His arms were tied to the bed rails. Needles were embedded in one of his wrists and tubes were extended from his wrist to machines by the bedside. The machines held bags of fluid that ran through the tubes into his body. One machine had a bellows type apparatus that gasped with a swishing noise every time it pushed air into the Prince's mouth piece. The other side of the bed had a heart monitor that showed waves of red and a bright light that lit up on every heartbeat. It was over whelming – swish, bleep, pause, swish, bleep, pause. The Prince's eyes were wide open but one could tell he was in the middle of a horrific battle. His body was shaking and thrashing around like he was trying to avoid being tortured.

Bending over his bed she gently kissed his forehead. She whispered in his ear – hardly able to get the words out of her constricted throat as she tried to stop her silent weeping.

"Roger, it's Orinda, your wife. We are in this together. I love you so much."

She felt a hand on her elbow.

"Mrs. Paulson, is there someone you can call? I can help you to the waiting room and you can come in every hour for a few minutes. We will monitor him and let you know if there are any changes."

She submitted to the suggestion.

In the waiting room, her trembling hands pulled her address book out of her purse. Soon she was weeping with her sister, then her pastor, then her good friend. They were on their way to be by her side. Jan and Pastor Merrill were at a conference at North Western College, a good drive away. She quickly posted a shout out on the campus prayer bulletin board. Sister Ilene found babysitters for her girls till her husband could come home. News spread quickly.

The ICU doctor entered the room and sat down beside her.

"Your husband has had a bleed in the brain. We have called Dr. Levitan. The seizures are normal at this point for this kind of trauma. He is on a ventilator to help him breathe. His platelets were very low so we are administering blood therapy. He may need several bags of blood. Do you know of anyone who can donate on his behalf? We don't want to take yours, though, as we want to keep you healthy so you can help us with his care. Do you have any questions?"

She was speechless, but inside she was shouting, "Stop these seizures? Is he going to die? What should I do? Will he be all right?"

She quietly came back into focus as the nurse announced, "You can see him now."

The ICU doctor took her by the elbow and walked with her back to his bedside. She quietly wept by his bedside, holding his shaking hand until she heard a familiar voice. It was Dr. Carl Christenson, the Chief of Staff at that time. He had received the call from Pastor and came downstairs to check on Roger and his condition. Still in his surgery gown, hair cover, and foot booties, she recognized her church Shepherd.

"Rindy, I'm afraid this is serious. ITP is not responding to medication and has found a weak blood vessel in his brain and it has ruptured. The next 72 hours are most important. If he survives this, there will be new things to consider. Who is here with you?"

"My sister is coming, and so is Pastor Bronco," she spouted out between sobs.

"I talked to Pastor and we would like to do an anointing of oil for his healing. As soon as Pastor arrives, I will come and get you. The Lord is with us."

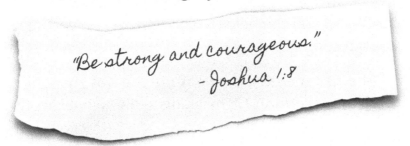

"Be strong and courageous."
— Joshua 1:8

When her sister arrived, the Lady updated her on all of the information. They went in together and prayed over the Prince together. He seemed to be a little less distressed – the seizures seemed to be less frequent. They were encouraged.

Dr. Skip Johnson showed up to check on Roger. He was carrying a little bundle.

"Look at this," he announced, "Jenna Johnson has just arrived. God is the giver of life, Rindy."

"Oh, how darling! How is Jan?"

"She is doing well. She sends her prayers for Roger and you."

The Lady mused, "How strange this moment. Here is beautiful new life in this valley of possible death. And God is involved with both. Oh Lord, help me to trust you!"

Dr. Christenson arrived again, this time in his doctor's coat. He questioned the nurses,

"Are you finished?"

They immediately left the bed side. Pastor gave the Lady a hug and then approached the Prince's bedside. Dr. Johnson stepped in, as well as two elders from our church. Dr. Christenson began the little service with prayer,

"Lord, YOU are the Great Physician. We ask you to bring healing to our brother Roger and restore him to health."

They poured a small amount of oil on his shaking forehead and continued in prayer. The Lady felt The Lord's presence at this solemn, holy moment.

By this time, evening had arrived as well as many "well wishers." Her sister was an excellent greeter. She updated them and saved the Lady the fatigue of repeating the sad story over and over again.

Escaping into the women's restroom, the Lady went into a stall, locked the door, and sat down on the seat. There she bore her heart to the Lord. Choking on her sobs, the tears cascading down her cheeks dripping on her lap, she cried out in a contrite prayer:

"Lord, don't let him die! I need him! I need him! Lord, how will I live without him? Lord, please don't let him die!"

And the Lord answered her prayer.

Chapter 18

The Three Doors

P arking her car in the hospital lot for her daily visit, she grabbed two bags – one for her school papers and the other just fun stuff.

"Hi Florence,"

She greeted the desk clerk as she briskly walked into the elevator. Without hesitation she pushed "2." It was so automatic. The doors opened smoothly, depositing her onto the second floor. She approached the desk of the charge nurse. Ruth Ann looked up and greeted her cheerfully,

"Hi Rindy, how are you?"

"I'm good. Any updates?"

"Well, both Dr. Christenson and Dr. Levitan came by this morning. Roger is still in a stable condition – no changes. Your friends, the couple who play guitar and sing came early this afternoon. The whole floor enjoyed their music. We are all benefiting from caring for Roger."

"Thanks," she chirped. "I know he's getting good care here at Unity."

With that, she headed for Room 205 where her Prince, her Sleeping Beauty was waiting. She slowly opened the door and slipped into the room. He was seated in a chair, no more machines and tubes except the nasal gastric tube to feed him and a catheter, of course.

"Hi Honey," she announced, "How are you today?"

As usual, there was no response. He stared straight ahead with his brown button eyes. It was like he was imprisoned inside his own body. She wondered if he was fighting to get out. She wondered if he was blind. Settling her belongings, she came and gave him a kiss on the forehead and sat on the arm rest of the recliner. She talked and talked and shared about her day. It felt good to talk to someone, even if he couldn't answer. Then she got to work on her "wake up the Prince" program.

"Rog, I brought you some things. Look at this doggy ball. I picked it up at the pet store – it's RED. Raise your eye brows if you can see the red ball."

He was familiar with the silly raise your eye brow game. As newlyweds they would communicate in public with their eye brows. One raise meant "I love you" and two raises meant "Let's go soon."

"Rog, can you feel the rubber prickles on the ball? Raise your eye brows for me if you can feel it."

"Hey, Rog, smell this! I got these smelly stickers from my first graders. This one is bubble gum. Can you smell it? Raise your eye brows for me."

On and on went the antics – with no response. KTIS, the local Christian radio station was on 24/7 and filled the air with familiar voices and songs of hope. As it played *God Will Make a Way when there is no other way*, she drank in the words. She was so thirsty for hope.

Just last week the hospital scheduled another staffing for Roger. This time she brought moral support – her sister and her SWORD (her Bible). Every staff member involved with Roger's care was there, seated at the BIG table waiting for her like knights at the round table: the physical therapist, the neurologist, the oncologist, the Chaplain, the dietitian, the hospital social worker, and Ruth Ann, the charge nurse. It made her shake inside with anticipation of doom.

The atmosphere was thick and ever so serious. They started with greetings. The Lady introduced her sister and the meeting began. Each department gave

Roger's specific physical update. And then the final diagnosis: "Continual Vegetation State."

She knew it was coming. Dr. Christenson, her church Shepherd, had taken her to lunch to prepare her for the realities of the situation. But this time there was more than just the diagnosis. They wanted her to do two things: look for a nursing home that she would be comfortable with and – for her mental health and financial protection – begin the divorce proceedings that they had suggested at their last meeting. She knew this was because they cared about her future. They had all become more than just professionals – they were kind friends. They loved her and her Prince. The Lady sought counsel from Pastor John Hartzell, their best man and Roger's Navigator mentor. John asked,

"What would Rog tell you to do?"

She mused a moment and then replied, "Go to God's Word."

And so, she did. Reviewing all the scriptures that Pastor John had shared with her, she prayerfully considered them – and now she was ready – confirmed in her mind the position her Lord would embrace.

Her mind returned to all the serious faces focused on her – she began:

"Roger and I have had a healthy marriage. We based our decisions together on God's Word. We knew God had brought us together and had a plan for our lives. We are living that plan. I cannot divorce Roger. I married him until death parts us, not until it's inconvenient. We based our marriage on scripture: "What, therefore, God hath joined together, let not man put asunder!" (Mark 10:9) And, since right now I am making the decisions for both of us, I lean on Numbers 30:2: "If a man vows a vow unto the Lord, or swears an oath to bind his soul with a bond, he shall not break his word."

There was no response. Dead silence was only broken by the sound of sniffles. As she got up to leave the room – everyone was dabbing their eyes. Her SWORD had slain the Villain. God had given her the strength for the battle. The Peace that He promises when we honor HIM came over her as a cloak of warm encouragement. Silently, she and her sister left for Roger's room.

There she refocused on her Sleeping Beauty – so still, so lovely, so precious. He seemed to sense the tension, and as she held his hand he seem to move his fingers on top of her grasp.

"He seems to be feeling for your wedding ring," her sister pointed out.

"Could he really understand what was going on?" she shared with her sister.

"I have had several one-sided conversations with him. I have also played the cassette multiple times."

She directly inserted a copy of their wedding cassette into the cassette player. It had everything – the music, the words. Nothing was left out.

"Rog, remember this? It's our wedding. Look at this picture, Roger. You are the Groom and I am the Bride. I am your wife, Mrs. Roger Paulson. I will never leave you! I will not divorce you! I will be there for whatever door God opens for us."

It seemed to the Lady that there were three huge, thick doors looming before her. The doors had no door knobs. Yes, it would be the Lord's choice. The first door opened to a miraculous, complete healing. Oh, Glory, how very wonderful that would be!!! The Prince and the Lady would tell everyone what the Lord had done. The Second Door led to a nursing home where the Prince would live out the rest of his life. The Lady already knew she would visit every day, just like she had done for the last eight months. And the Third door entered into Eternity – living with the Lord forever – completely healed in a perfect way.

"Oh Lord," she prayed, "Help me to Trust you! I surrender to your Sovereignty."

Chapter 19

The Tap at the Window

The Lady was on the phone with her principal.

"Dr. Switzer, this is Rindy. May I have a sub today? I am not sick, I just can't get myself together."

"Well, sometimes we aren't physically sick, but our minds just need to rest," began her understanding principal. "By all means, take the day off. And greet that husband of yours. We are in prayer for you both."

"Thanks," responded the Lady and placed the phone into its cradle.

"Thank you, Lord, for such a caring principal," she prayed.

Many times her principal, Dr. Switzer, had taken over her classroom at short notice allowing her to rush to the office for a hospital phone call. Hard decisions had to be made on the spot.

"His platelets are very low, shall we give him a blood transfusion since you have stopped all medications?" the matter-of-fact nurse recited.

"They are thinking of moving him today to the Veterans Hospital. Would that be all right?" the nurse inquired.

"Only if they take the responsibility of his life during the transfer. I do NOT want him moved unless I am there," the Lady firmly responded.

She had become strong and direct.

As she laid back in bed and pulled the covers up she realized how drained and dehydrated she was from crying. She was limp from fatigue and not even sure if she could make the drive to the Veteran's Hospital on the other side of town. At least it was financially helpful as all of their insurance monies were gone. She began to backtrack. Sister Kenney Rehabilitation Center had tried to work with him, but the brain damage was so severe and the wicked ITP disease interfered with the treatments.

After eight and a half months, she agreed to the move him to Veteran's Hospital. He could only be accepted if they would be allowed to do experimental brain surgery and put in a shunt to drain the fluid off the brain. Three times, the Lady got a substitute teacher and the surgery was scheduled. Three times it was aborted because his platelets were in the danger level. Medical bleeding would take his life. The Lady had shared with the doctors that she and Roger were not afraid of his death. They did not want to block it from happening, BUT they did NOT want to remove his feeding tube or TAKE his life in any other way! They would wait on the Lord. Even if it meant financial disaster.

It seemed so strange that his coma had lifted but he was still so unable to function. Her thoughts were gnawing:

"Could he see? Could he hear? Was he still inside that sleeping body?"

A few times she had been shocked. The TV was on in the room and the announcer was sharing the tragic death of Princess Grace of Monaco.

The Prince announced, "Oh No!"

He had written the royal couple in 1974 to ask for a copy of their coat-of-arms. This was given to the Lady's sister and brother-in law, who just happened to have the same last name.

Then there was the time the Prince said to his beloved, "You are an angel."

Excited that he created a sentence, she ran to the nurse's station to report the news. They rejoiced together. She cherished those words in her heart. He never spoke again.

The phone rang, interrupting her silent thoughts. It was her good friend, Judy Chudek.

"Can I go with you today to see Roger?" she cheerfully asked.

Many times she had joined the Lady and been such an encourager and prayer warrior. They knew each other well as Judy and John were part of her church Agape Bible Study group. Several of the couples in that group embraced her with love and care – the Magnasons, the Bruders, the Kramers. They had her for dinner, anytime, shoveled her winter walkways, even did her laundry. Howie Rexstad brought his sons after a deep blizzard and dug out her patio garage entrance. The Lady was told to carry a suitcase in the trunk of her car so she could stay overnight when necessary. Sometimes, Roger's life was a thread away from Heaven and her Agape Group did not want her to be alone if she got a call during the night. They were a bulwark of faith as the Lady walked through this "valley of the shadow of death."

She finished dressing and sat down on the toilet seat. She held her head in her hands, elbows on her knees, and sobbed unto the Lord. Tears cascaded down her knees dripping on the floor. An avalanche of pain poured from her heart.

"Lord, please take him home. I cannot stand the agony of seeing him slowly die in front of me. He has been through so much suffering. Please, please, Lord, take him home."

The door bell rang and faithful Judy was standing there ready to give a hug. They drove to the hospital with simple chatter. It had become more than just a visit and update of the Prince's condition. Everyone knew he was near death. The relentless, wicked Idiopathic thrombo cyctopenia had loomed into an unsurmountable monster that the Prince could not fight any more. His strength was gone and every breath was an effort. The nurses administered comfort medicine and at request would give him a dose of some kind of medicine to keep him from throwing up blood. His arms and legs were full of petechiae and he just couldn't respond to anyone in the room.

The Lady began as usual to read him Scripture and sing their special songs – especially *Praise the Savior*. All six verses were still in her heart and mind:

> *Praise the Savior, ye who know Him,*
>
> *who can tell how much you owe him,*
>
> *Gladly let us render to Him*
>
> *all we are and have.*

Jesus is the name that charms us,

He for conflict fits and arms us.

Nothing moves, nor nothing harms us,

While we trust in Him.

Trust in Him...

Every verse was meant for this special occasion.

She called her sister and she and her brother-in-law arrived early evening. As they stood around his bed, they took turns quoting scripture.

"The Lord has taken away thy judgments, he hath cast our thine enemy: The King of Israel, even the Lord, is in the midst of thee, thou shalt not see evil anymore."
— Zephaniah 3:15

The Lady's last words were read from Isaiah.

"Fear not, for I have redeemed thee; I have called thee by thy name; thou art mine. When thou passest through the waters, I will be with thee; and through the rivers, they shall not overflow thee; when thou walkest through the fire, thou shall not be burned, neither shall the flame kindle upon thee. For I am the Lord thy God, the Holy One of Israel, thy Savior."

— Isaiah 43:1-3

As the four people held hands around the Prince's bed and sang *Blest Be the Tie That Binds*, a gentle wind came from nowhere and a twig tapped at the window pane. The Prince heaved a deep breath like he was preparing for a new adventure.

And he was gone.

Epilogue

O f course, Roger's passing was not the end of the story. While his death was excruciating for those who knew and loved him, he finished his journey in the arms of his Lord and Savior, Jesus Christ. He will live eternally with HIM.

"Looking unto Jesus, the Author and Finisher of our faith." Hebrews 12:2a

Deep gratitude to all of the doctors, nurses, and staff from

Unity Hospital

Sister Kenney Rehabilitation Center

Minnesota Veteran's Hospital

who valiantly tried to save Roger's life and always treated him with dignity.

Thank you!

Orinda Paulson Koukal

Before You Go

*I*f you found this book to be valuable, would you please consider leaving your feedback on Amazon.com, with your library, or bookseller of choice? It would be greatly appreciated. Your reviews make this book more visible for those who might not otherwise discover it or need it.